101 WAYS TO START YOUR OWN BUSINESS

101 WAYS TO START YOUR OWN BUSINESS

Second Edition

Christine Ingham

KOGAN PAGE

First published in 1992
Second edition published 1997

Kogan Page Limited
120 Pentonville Road
London N1 9JN

British Library Cataloguing in Publication Data

A CIP record for this book is available from the British Library.

ISBN 0-7494-2186-X

Printed and bound in Great Britain by Clays Ltd, St Ives plc
Typeset by Saxon Graphics Ltd, Derby

Contents

Introduction: Positive Moves into Self-Employment

Going into business can offer you an incredibly exciting challenge. The pay-offs can be high and job satisfaction enormous. It makes one wonder why everyone isn't doing it.

Perhaps what frightens some people is the risk element. Being employed by someone else appears to avoid that and has, in the past, made for a more secure working life. Sadly, as many people who face redundancy find out, that idea has now become redundant itself. So now we must ask the question: Which is more risky – being in a job where you may find yourself out of work next week, or becoming self-employed where you manage and minimise the risks yourself?

A frequently quoted figure is that 90 per cent of businesses fail within the first five years of trading. What they don't tell you is that 80 per cent of those people who become self-employed *stay* self-employed. In the USA they back this up and say that you're not a true entrepreneur until you've had three business failures!

But the possibility of failure can be minimised. A successful business depends largely on good planning and thorough groundwork. There are many useful books currently available which explain in detail how to set up your own business. Your local library should be able to help. Make use of the advice, especially if you don't have a business background. It can help to make the vitally important planning stage that much easier for you.

In the meantime, here are some basic pointers to help raise your awareness of some things you need to consider.

You

Are you fully aware of all your skills, expertise, aptitudes and experience? Becoming familiar with your own personal resources and limitations is important and needs a fair bit of honest self-assessment. Kogan Page's book *The Entrepreneur's Complete Self-Assessment Guide* by Douglas A Gray can help and is highly recommended. You may highlight gaps in some knowledge or skill areas. Plan to fill them through training or by finding what you lack in someone else. Then once you are fully aware of your personal resources you can plan to make effective use of them.

Try to clarify your own personal reasons for setting up in business and what your personal and business objectives are. Knowing why you are doing something and having your aims clear in your mind makes the planning much easier. Running a business is hard work and especially so if you intend to operate as a sole trader (ie working on your own), so your motivation must be very high; high enough to see you through the inevitable trying and difficult periods which all businesses experience from time to time.

You can only feel motivated when totally clear about why you're doing what you're doing, and what your sights are set on: you have to have a vision. Otherwise, do you think you will be able to work the long hours, do the jobs which you don't like doing (sweeping the floor at the end of a day's business; seeing to the accounts) and live for a week on just £5 and a creative attitude towards a can of beans? Your business idea must motivate you, make you excited, get the sap rising every time you think about it.

Similarly, if you have a family it helps to have their full commitment to the idea as well. Facing a challenging day at work is one thing; to be faced with unhelpful or resentful attitudes at home afterwards is another.

Plan for business

At the research and planning stage it is vital to take off the rose-tinted specs. If the figures say that it would cost £100 to make a widget which you know would sell for only £50, be honest with yourself and accept them. No jiggling of those figures, hiding additional costs or 'forgetting' to include the wage bill will make the reality any different. Keep those rose-tints firmly at bay.

Let's have a look at the areas of research you need to look into:

Costing What will it cost to produce your widget, or whatever product or service you intend to have as the basis for your business? Include the cost of premises, equipment hire, running costs (like electricity, telephones), supplies, wages, your drawings (ie salary/wage). Think of everything – and this means everything, right down to the last paper clip – which goes towards making and selling your product. Then add on an allowance for price increases.

Pricing Consider what price the market can stand as well as what people's expectations are. Look at your competitors. Can you compete with them on price alone – or can you offer something else, like a better quality of service? Remember that the price of goods can be too low as well as too high.

Customers Who are they? Have a very clear picture in your mind since this will affect your product or service design, your business image, where and how you advertise, pricing and so on.

How many of them are there? Once you know who your customers are, you are in a position to find out how many of them there are by researching for figures at your local library. Ask the librarian to help. There are many sources available which he or she will help you find and use.

Marketing How are you going to reach your customers and let them know you're there? You may have a very good product which potentially has a big market, but can you get to it? What is your weekly/monthly/yearly marketing strategy going to be?

Work out your business image. Will it be upmarket and trendy or classic and chintzy; down to earth and practical or zappy and alternative? How will your merchandise be packaged? What's your business name, and does it work with or against your overall image?

Where will you advertise and how much will it cost? Remember that this will rarely be a one-off charge. Advertising needs to appear regularly to be effective.

Projected Sales How many can you sell? Be honest about this. Think about seasonal fluctuations and other factors which may affect your sales pattern throughout the year. For example, a widget sold at football matches will have a different sales pattern from other widgets designed as Christmas novelties. Find out about your market and how many people would realistically buy – then be a touch pessimistic.

Finance With your costing, pricing and estimated sales figures to hand you can then look more honestly at the finance involved: what you need to get started; how much immediate cash you have available; how much other people are willing/able to contribute; how much security you have to borrow against. One of the main reasons for business failures is underfunding – not having enough money to start off with – so make sure you don't fall into that trap.

Find out if you will have to pay VAT – not all businesses do; it depends on the sort of business you operate as well as turnover. Contact your local Customs and Excise office for information. And what about National Insurance? How much tax are you likely to have to pay – and when?

Find out about how to draw up a cash flow and a profit and loss sheet. Unbridled enthusiasm may be carrying you into euphoric states of optimism but an honestly constructed cash-flow will show you whether you're on to a real winner or not.

Market Research So it all looks rosy on paper and the argument in favour looks overwhelmingly convincing. You still need to carry out some market research. It's important to find out what people's attitudes really are towards your new-style widget. Would they be likely to buy one, five, ten, or none? Do they like the colour? What do they need from the service that no one else is giving? Will your product satisfy their needs? You've gone to all the trouble of identifying your target audience, now you need to find out whether they'll be interested or not. Carrying out *thorough* market research and being honest with yourself about the results is vital. It can save the anguish of starting a business doomed to failure simply because you didn't find out beforehand that people prefer widgets which are red and have a handle on them instead.

Workplace Think carefully about this. Perhaps the hobby which is now going to form the basis for your business has been happily housed in the back room for years. Will husband/wife/playful pet/baby be quite so happy so see full-scale production oozing into each and every room? If working from home is the best way for you, still check leases for prohibitive clauses as well as council regulations. Similarly, business premises need to be vetted for their usage and if you're planning any sort of building work to accommodate business activities you must check with your local council beforehand.

Keep your eye on the future and consider how easily the business could expand in the premises you have in mind. Moving is disruptive and costly, especially if you find yourself bound to long leases. Make sure the premises are right.

Local Business Links will help to point you in the right direction for finding suitable premises and advise you on any available grants to help with refurbishment.

Selling Can you sell? Can you close a deal? Do you know what that means? Selling could form the basis for a whole book in itself, so if you answered an honest 'No', and you cannot afford to employ someone else to do it for you, it is probably a good idea to start reading as much as you can about it, and 'phone your local Training and Enterprise Council (TEC) or Local Enterprise Company (LEC) in Scotland and speak to their enterprise team or small business unit for information about locally sponsored courses.

Being a good salesperson could make or break your business, so be sure to update your skills if you know they are lacking in this vitally important area.

Controls

So the business is up and off and you're as high as the proverbial kite. You've done the groundwork, proved it was a viable proposition, launched the business and made your first sale. Wonderful! Congratulations!

But after a month how will you know if you are still on target? Which debtors haven't paid their bills yet? What will be the real effect of accepting that enormous order which seems just too good to turn down? Overtrading (taking on too much work which can adversely affect a weak cash flow) is another common pitfall in eager new enterprises.

All businesses need controls. They enable you to weather the trickier times and perhaps help you to foresee, and take measures to avoid, others. Stock control is an obvious one but think as well about such things as how to monitor production and late payment of bills by customers. Remember that you are in business to make money, not just to make and supply widgets.

Keep tight control over the business and know what's going on where, especially on the money side. If necessary, take professional advice from your accountant, bank manager or business adviser. Spotting problems before they get out of hand will help you to avoid troublesome times.

A helping hand

There are many sources of help available to assist you in starting your own business. Begin by taking a trip to your local library and find out:

- Names and addresses of relevant trade associations.
- Your local Business Links addresses – a one-stop shop for business help and advice.
- Address of your local Chamber of Commerce.
- Books about setting up and running your own business.

Also:

- Visit branches of as many different banks as possible. Most have free information packs about setting up in business.
- Your local TEC, LEC or Business Links have many free publications.
- You may be eligible for financial assistance from the government if, for example, you are currently unemployed, disabled, or an ex-offender. If you are under 25 you may also be able to apply to the Prince's Trust for financial and other assistance as well – ask at your local Business Link, TEC or LEC for details. See also page 183.
- Your bank may have an Enterprise Unit which may be able to offer advice. Ask local branches where the nearest one is.

These few pages have touched only lightly on some of the aspects which you need to consider in detail before going into business. By finding out more, researching and planning well, you can avoid many of the pitfalls which assail other new enterprises. Yours needn't be one of them.

So, what's your dream business going to be?

Way 1 Accommodation

Are you a home owner? If so, you could already have a potential business to hand. Your house is an asset, but it could also be providing you with an income.

There are many different ways in which to let rooms: short term, bed and breakfast, long term or lodging (ie providing meals).

And, of course, there are different markets to tap into: travellers, students, holiday makers, foreign students, people on business, as well as those people simply looking for somewhere to put down roots.

But before making a final decision, think carefully about your location. It will be useless targeting the business market if you live in a small backwater. Are you close to a tourist area, business complex, college/university, or are you on a through route for travellers? Contact organisations and businesses which may need temporary or long-term accommodation for visitors, students or relocated employees.

All this research will help you make the best decision about how to rent. It will also help you to work out how best to advertise: by word of mouth, in newsagents' windows, college noticeboards, in local papers, through your Chamber of Commerce, in foreign newspapers or through your local tourist board. Match your advertising to your market and start to make your asset work for you.

This will appeal if

- You enjoy meeting people.
- You like housework.
- You're organised.

Advantages (depending on the type of letting)

- A regular income for relatively little work.
- Free time to follow other pursuits (even start another business).
- You can choose your customers.

Disadvantages (again, depending on the type of letting)

- Loss of privacy.
- Intermittent business with bed and breakfast accommodation.
- You may be affected by peak and off-peak seasons.

Future possibilities

- Build extensions to accommodate more guests.
- Move out of the property and rent it out as a whole or convert it into flats.
- Buy other properties or ongoing businesses.

Addresses

British Tourist Authority, Thames Tower, Blacks Road, London W6 9EL; 0181-846 9000.

British Federation of Hotel, Guest House and Self-Catering Associations, 5 Sandycroft Road, Blackpool, Lancs FY1 2RY; 01253 352683

Publications
Profitable Letting, Robert B Davies; Fourmat Publishing 1989
Landlord and Tenant, J M Male; 4th edition; Macdonald and Evans, 1995
Starting a Bed and Breakfast Business, British Tourist Authority (see above)
Running Your Own Bed and Breakfast, Elizabeth Gundry; Piatkus Books, 1989

Way 2 Antiques

People's abiding interest in antiques provides a ready-made market for a business in this fascinating field.

You could start off with just a humble market stall at weekends, or you may decide to sell to other dealers. Take time to visit their shops and find out who collects what, then you will know what to look out for.

But whichever way you decide to work, it is best to specialise, become an 'expert' and make it easier to spot those good finds.

Remember too that while not officially antiques, there are lots of other collectable items in which you could specialise; for example, posters, Matchbox toys or even pop memorabilia.

Where to find your stock? Mainly at auction. A few boxes of goods can be picked up cheaply enough and could produce some interesting pieces to start you off. The auctions you attend depend on what you want to deal in, and the level at which you want to 'operate': up or down market. They're all listed in the weekly *Antiques Trade Gazette*.

So, if you like beautiful objects, are willing to put in a fair amount of learning, and have a good eye for a bargain, antiques could provide the opening for you into self-employment.

This will appeal if

- You have a good memory for facts, figures and faces.
- You're good at research.
- You enjoy travelling around.
- You have a good eye for spotting saleable items.

Advantages

- You can start off in a small, part-time way.
- You can build up your stock over a long period to avoid an initial, large investment.
- Lots of variety.
- Good mark-up on items.

Disadvantages

- Storage if you want to handle large items.
- Requires transport.
- You need access to funds to buy stock, even if you do spread it over a number of months.
- Sales may be intermittent at first.

Future possibilities

- Move into shop premises.
- Learn how to renovate pieces and offer this as an ancillary service.
- Deal up-market, ie in more rare and expensive items.
- Investigate international markets.

Addresses

British Antique Dealers' Association, 20 Rutland Gate, London SW7 1BD; 0171-589 4128

London & Provincial Antique Dealers' Association, 535 King's Road, London SW10 0SZ; 0171-823 3511

Publications
Antiques Trade Gazette (weekly)
Guide to the Antique Shops of Britain (annual)
How to Make Money Out of Antiques, Judith Miller; Mitchell Beazley, 1996

Way 3 Architectural salvage

Homeowners and property developers fall into two categories: modernisers and restorers. Modernisers like to buy a property and remove all trace of original features which don't fit in with their more up-to-date tastes and contemporary lifestyles. Out go old fireplaces; in come central heating systems. Down come old brick walls; up go plasterboard partitions.

Restorers, on the other hand, prefer to keep the enamelled bath, kitchen range, and turn of the century tiles. And what previous owners have removed is now hunted down so that reinstatement can complete their restoration plan, returning the property to its former glory.

Architectural salvagers take advantage of this never-ending cycle of disposal by the modernisers and reinstatement by the restorers. One is only too glad to rid themselves of items which stand in the way of their modernising programme; the other is desperately in search of those very pieces which have been discarded. Many salvage items can command high prices, either because of their scarcity or because of new trends.

Most important in this business is having suitable storage space. Architectural salvage tends to be big and heavy: columns, marble fireplaces, cast iron items. An old warehouse is ideal. Transport suitable for the job is also important, and consideration must be given to lifting and moving, especially heavy items.

Link up with builders and demolition firms who would be

happy to have someone save them the trouble of disposal. Stock can be marketed through renovation specialists, interior designers and even garden centres – as well as to homeowners keen on DIY.

This will appeal if

- You have an interest in buildings and antiques.
- You have a good eye for spotting marketable pieces.
- You are fit – if you intend to physically handle pieces.
- You can get on with a wide range of people.

Advantages

- Stock can be acquired cheaply.
- New trends can often boost the value of items already in stock.
- Restoring original features to properties is popular.
- Trade customers are easy to target.

Disadvantages

- Space – could be a costly overhead.
- Building up stock levels may take time.
- Additional staff needed – for moving stock or dealing with customers.
- A heavy goods vehicle is vital.

Future possibilities

- Reproduce and sell copies of popular items.
- Import and/or export items abroad.
- Set up operations in other countries.
- Specialise in a particular range of items, eg garden monuments.
- Set up an advisory service for renovators.
- Offer a fitting, renovation and design service.
- Hire items: to film and television companies; conference organisers; events organisers; photographers etc.

Publications
Salvo (monthly)
Salvo News (weekly)

Way 4 Bicycle repairs

As people are becoming more environmentally aware, those who can are handing in the car keys and changing over to pedal power. And with this increase in the number of bicycles on the road you have a correspondingly expanding market in bicycle repairs. It's a ready-made opportunity for you to turn to your advantage.

You could start small by travelling to where repairs are needed, similar to how the RAC and AA operate. In this way you get around the problem of finding workshop premises.

If this is the way you want to start out, think about how you're going to find your customers, or conversely how they are going to find you. Advertise widely through bike retail outlets, 'alternative' and bicycle magazines, local papers and Yellow Pages. Car owners are always having leaflets left on their windscreens. Could you do something similar with bikes to advertise your services? And don't overlook yourself as a vehicle for carrying advertising. Have some T-shirts and outdoor clothing printed with your business name and telephone number (a mobile telephone is essential). It will also help to reinforce your professional image when your customers see you kitted out.

Although you may repair all types and makes of bicycle, you could also specialise: children's bikes, mountain bikes, racing bikes, or any other type. Do some market research and find out what the demands are in your area.

A successful business depends on the size of its market. Here you have an expanding one, just waiting for you to move into. So – on your bike!

This will appeal if

- You're practical.
- You enjoy bike riding.
- You're a quick worker.
- You're reliable.
- You know how to repair bikes – or can go into partnership with someone who does.

Advantages

- Low cost start-up.
- Few overheads to start.

- It's an expanding market.
- Good cash flow set-up.

Disadvantages

- Working in all weathers.
- Will take time to become established.
- As a small trader your prices may be higher since you may not be able to buy parts in bulk.

Future possibilities

- Acquire premises.
- Offer a security marking service.
- Offer a maintenance service.
- Deal in second-hand bikes.
- Sell ancillary lines, clothes and insurance.
- Establish operations in other locations.
- Expand into a nationwide network.
- Franchise the operation.

Publications
Cycling Today (monthly)
Cycle Trader (monthly)
Sloane's New Bicycle Maintenance Manual; Simon & Schuster, 1995

Way 5 Bodyguard service

Acting as a bodyguard requires more than mere muscle and brawn. Close-protection operatives need to be intelligent, alert – and trained. Most who enter this field have military training behind them, or are ex-police who are familiar with the full repertoire of techniques for taking care of their client, and themselves.

Although the work can be lucrative, you need to be able to demonstrate you can 'deliver the goods'. Clients have a lot at stake, so it is understandable that their expectations will be high. Good credentials are vital to making a successful in-road into this profession, especially since there are well-established players in the field who you'll be up against.

People requiring the services of a bodyguard include visiting dignitaries, wealthy business people, pop stars, actors, celebrities, and possibly their close relatives as well. Past personal experience or contacts in any of these fields will help enormously, not only in finding clients, but also in understanding the different circles in which people move and the potential threats to their security and protection.

Offering a full, round-the-clock protection service will mean hiring additional staff, either permanent or on a freelance basis. On the other hand you may decide to restrict contracts to ones which are time-limited, such as providing a protective escort to and from a special event or location. This sort of work includes one-off events but can also be on a regular basis.

Despite what the films may lead us to believe, close-protection work involves little drama and excitement (if you're doing your job properly) and much checking, double-checking, re-checking, and then checking again. If it's gun-wielding, car-chasing, shoot-out action you want, check out Way 29 instead – Film making.

This will appeal if

- You have a suitable background and the necessary skills.
- You are fit and alert (if you intend to carry out the work yourself).
- You have good interpersonal skills.
- You have an eye for detail, good levels of concentration – and can handle standing around being bored.

Advantages

- Lucrative work.
- Low overheads.
- Offers a good way of building on existing skills and knowledge.
- Offers possibilities for expansion.

Disadvantages

- Can involve unsociable hours.
- Stressful and potentially dangerous work.
- Difficult to run without additional staff.

Future possibilities

- Expand into private investigation work (see Way 72).
- Develop other security guard services, eg guarding commercial premises.
- Establish a training school and become the by-word in producing quality personnel.
- Develop a consultancy service.
- Use your knowledge as the basis for a novel.

Addresses

British Security Industry Association, Security House, Barbourne Road, Worcester WR1 1RS; 01905 21464

International Professional Security Association, 292a Torquay Road, Paignton, Devon TQ3 2EZ; 01803 554849

Way 6 Book search service

As publishers become more cost efficient, many have begun to cut their backlist of published books in order to reduce warehousing costs. Besides providing the book remainder trade with business, it also presents another opportunity: finding out-of-print books for people.

Find your customers by advertising in book collector magazines or scanning advertisers' 'Wants' lists. Advertise your service in local papers, student magazines, special interest magazines, your local library, or even your local bookshop – negotiating a commission for them if necessary.

Find the books by typing your own list of 'Wants' and circulating it to second-hand bookshops and other book search businesses, and scan the 'For Sale' lists in the trade magazines.

This is a business where specialising certainly makes sense. In this way you can offer a much more efficient service, develop your own clientele and forge close working links with suppliers. It also makes it easier to spot what you're looking for when you do go out and about. You can start to build your own stock of books, in your specialist field, and in this way have other book search services coming to you for business.

Price your sales to make sure all costs are covered, including advertising, postage and packing, and of course your time. And with a little bit of hard work and organisation you could soon be successfully trading full time.

This will appeal if

- You enjoy books.
- You're good at research and enjoy investigative work.
- You're organised.
- You have a good telephone manner – a lot of the work will involve the phone.

Advantages

- Low cost start-up.
- Few overheads – you can operate from home.
- Can be started off part time.
- Good mark-up on items.

Disadvantages

- Could take time to develop the large client list which you need to be profitable.

Future possibilities

- Trade up-market, eg dealing in first editions.
- Acquire premises and develop a general second-hand book business as well.
- Once in premises, stock new as well as second-hand books.
- Broaden your specialist base; if necessary by buying in specialist knowledge.
- Tap into the international market.

Publications
Book Collector (quarterly)
Bookdealer (weekly). On subscription from Werner Shaw Ltd, Suite 34, 26 Charing Cross Road, London, WC2H 0DH; 0171-240 5890
Book and Magazine Collector (monthly)
AAB's British Book Search Services Leaflet (free). Magna Graecia's Publishers, PO Box 342, Oxford OX1 1NN; 01865 792610

Way 7 Box designs

Look around. See how many box shapes there are in your everyday life. When you notice how many, you will begin to realise the versatility in the shape and how it could lead to a number of business opportunities.

Using basic carpentry skills you can take this simple shape and adapt it into: bed bases, display systems, room dividers, desk struts, perhaps sold in kit form (cheaper in labour, transport and storage costs). Rectangular shapes lend themselves to linen boxes, storage boxes, toy boxes. Smaller shapes turn into spice boxes, jewellery boxes, pencil cases. Have a brainstorming session to think of others. How might you decorate them?

Consider how to sell. Do you supply shops or retail them yourself? Could you run a market stall instead of a shop, or sell them from your workshop? If you're going to make one-off handcrafted designs, you could consider craft fairs as well.

A rider should be added which will help your marketing. The consumer's awareness about green issues is now firmly in place. Choose woods which come from sustainable sources – and advertise the fact that you do. Don't leave it up to the consumer to decide whether you do or not.

So, by using basic skills and adapting a simple concept you could start to build a sound business.

This will appeal if

- You have some basic carpentry skills – or are able to pick them up.
- You enjoy practical work.
- You're a quick worker.
- You have a good eye for detail.
- You have design skills.

Advantages

- An easy business to test out first with samples.
- You can start part time.
- You can start with small items and a limited product range to keep initial costs down.
- It's an adaptable business concept.

Disadvantages

- Investment in tools, materials and a work space needed.
- Could be boring – 26 jewellery boxes, all the same design, by Thursday!
- Time – if you intend to make, market and sell by yourself.

Future possibilities

- Invest in plant to speed production and reduce labour costs.
- Open a retail outlet (The Box Shop?), selling boxes in different materials: cardboard, raffia, basketwork etc.
- Establish outlets in other towns/cities.
- Investigate export possibilities.

Publications
Woodworking News (monthly)
Making Wooden Boxes, Jeff Green; David & Charles, 1996
Making Small Wooden Boxes, James A. Jacobson; Sterling, 1996
Marvellous Wooden Boxes You Can Make, Jeff Greef; Betterway, 1996

Way 8 Business support service

Self-employed people are in a difficult position. They need to accept as much paying work as possible yet also deal with the non-paying workload, like letter writing and book-keeping.

This presents a valuable business opportunity for you.

Your support service could offer not only to solve their immediate problem by providing that essential support service, but also help to increase their efficiency and profitability.

Think about what you could offer: telephone message service, appointment booking system, fax service, meeting rooms, word processing, a postal address. Tie this in with your market research to find the likely uptake, which services would be most needed, as well as what the competition (if any) is offering.

Decide whether to operate on a contract basis only (good for your cash flow), or whether to offer an item-by-item service (costly to invoice and bad for your cash flow).

And how do you find those customers? You could advertise in

local papers, or mail potential customers direct. All businesses need paper clips and writing paper, so you could ask your local stationer if they would be willing to insert leaflets with purchases, perhaps for a small fee. Ditto for local print shops. You could also have a mutually beneficial agreement with solicitors and accountants, introducing new clients to each other, perhaps on a commission basis.

But essentially the success of the business will depend not only on finding the customers but on keeping them. Efficiency must be your by-word, along with reliability, and if you can offer a high quality service this could be the venture which ensures your own business success.

This will appeal if

- You have some clerical skills and experience.
- You're highly organised.
- You're reliable.
- You have good telephone and communication skills.

Advantages

- Regular work once your customer base is established.
- Good cash flow set-up.
- Varied work.

Disadvantages

- Requires investment for equipment.
- You are tied to the office.
- Overheads, if operating from premises.

Future possibilities

- Recruit additional staff as the work-flow increases.
- Market ancillary services (see Way 14 and Way 44).
- Establish branches in other areas.
- See Way 62.
- Offer an advisory service on setting up offices and administrative systems.
- Develop a temping agency.

Way 9 Buying and renovating properties

Fortunes can be made and lost in property. It's a fluctuating market as many people over the years have found out. But with sound planning and advice it can yield excellent returns.

For this business you need access to funds either from savings, selling your existing property, through borrowing, or through setting up a syndicate where members contribute a percentage of the costs. In this way the risks are shared – but so are the profits. Auctions, held by estate agents, are perhaps the best place for picking up suitable properties.

Whichever way you choose to operate, you need to have each project fully costed before making any financial commitment. Not only do you need a surveyor's help here, you also need some sound advice from an accountant. He or she will look at the proposal objectively and help you to assess whether the return will be high enough to make it worth your while.

You may have the building experience and expertise to do the work yourself and moving into the property while you complete the work can massively increase your returns. But you really do need to know what you're doing and understand the various building and health and safety regulations.

This is a high investment business and things can go wrong. But with good professional advice and a realistic appraisal of each proposed project you could find that this is the way to build your business success.

This will appeal if

- You're good at seeing the potential in buildings.
- You're good at negotiating.
- You have some experience of the building trade if you intend to do the work yourself.
- You're good at delegation.

Advantages

- Potentially high returns.
- You needn't do the work yourself.
- You can share the costs by forming a syndicate.
- At present, you can retain the freehold.

Disadvantages

- High cost investment.
- It's a fluctuating market.
- They're long-term projects.
- Irregular income.

Future possibilities

- If you started by doing the work yourself, pay builders to do it.
- Move into more expensive areas.
- Take on larger developments.
- Move into commercial re-developments.

Addresses

Building Centres. Regionally located; consult your local telephone directory.

Building Research Establishment, Bucknalls Lane, Garston, Watford, Herts WD2 7JR; 01923 894040

Federation of Master Builders, 14-15 Gt James Street, London WC1N 3DP; 0171-242 7586

Publications
Property Bid List (fortnightly)
Building (weekly)
Streetwise Guide to Renovating Your Home, Alison Cork; Piatkus, 1996

Way 10 Buying an existing business

You don't have to think of a new, original idea to go into business. If you know which type of business you would like to run, why not consider buying a going concern?

It has lots of advantages, not least of which is the opportunity you have to see the business in action. This means you can assess it before making a financial commitment. With new ventures you don't have that chance.

Ask your solicitor or business adviser, and your accountant, to have a good look over both the premises and the books. Check out the reason for selling, the history of the business, its competitors, new legislation which might affect its future viability, as well as things like its location. (Is the town centre moving? Are there new developments close by?)

If it proves to be just an ailing business, can you show how you would hope to turn it around? Do you have the necessary skills? What ideas would you have to improve it – better marketing, diversification, specialisation, improved training?

Be realistic. Some businesses are simply in the wrong place at the wrong time and will fail no matter what you or anyone else does. If you think that is the case, bide your time, hold on to your purse strings and wait for a more promising venture. There are certainly lots to be had.

This will appeal if

- Starting from scratch doesn't appeal to you.
- You're quick to fit in and adjust.
- You're good at problem solving (if it has any to be solved).
- You're lacking business ideas of your own.

Advantages

- You can see before you buy.
- You can easily assess its viability.
- The hard work in setting up a business has already been done.

Disadvantages

- There may be hidden reasons why the business is being sold.
- Requires high investment.
- Maintaining customer and staff confidence may be difficult.

Future possibilities

Depending on what type of business is involved you could:

- Expand the customer base.
- Extend the range of goods/services.
- Acquire allied 'supply' businesses.
- Establish a nationwide chain.
- Sell the business once it has become well established and profitable, re-invest the profit … or retire to the Bahamas!

Publications
Daltons Weekly
Buying and Selling a Business, Robert F Klueger; Wiley, 1996

Way 11 Cake design

Just think of all the many different events we celebrate besides birthdays, weddings and anniversaries. Businesses celebrate retirements, the best salesperson of the year and selling another million widgets. Societies and clubs regularly hold celebratory functions. And what about competition winners, 'welcome homes' and 'passing that driving test', not to mention the celebration of religious festivals?

The opportunities for a business in cake design are enormous.

Decide if you want to offer a speciality, perhaps in classic cake, novel or personalised cake design. Build a photographic portfolio of each creation to show to potential buyers, and if possible accompany them with references from satisfied customers.

And how do you find those customers? You could advertise regularly in local papers, do a leaflet drop to households, and mail businesses, clubs and societies direct. Contact catering firms too, and cake shops or delicatessens who could earn a commission from passing customers on to you.

Make your service special: a free delivery service; free plates and napkins (specially designed and printed with your name) and free forks as well. You could even offer a service on which wine to serve with each cake.

Celebrations are special occasions. By offering a high quality service you can make them even more special and also create a promising business for yourself.

This will appeal if

- You're imaginative.
- You're organised and reliable.
- You have some artistic ability.
- You like a challenge – how would *you* design a cake for the early retirement of a golf-loving dipsomaniac?

Advantages

- Could start in your spare time.
- Good cash flow set-up: payment in advance or on delivery.
- Highly enjoyable work.
- Can also offer to supply shops with standard cakes to help maintain regular work flow.

Disadvantages

- It could take time to become established.
- Need to apply for a food-handling licence from your local Environmental Health Officer.
- Irregular work flow.

Future possibilities

- Acquire shop premises. Sell books and baking supplies – all to do with cake making.
- Franchise the shops.
- Develop a full party planning service (see Way 64).
- Develop a full catering service.
- Develop your own range of cake decorations.

Publications
Cake Decoration (monthly)
Jane Asher's Book of Cake Decorating Ideas, Jane Asher; BBC, 1993
Master Bakers' Handbook and Buyers' Guide. An annual directory published by the Turret Group plc
Jane Asher's Party Cakes, Jane Asher; Pelham, 1985
Various books by Mary Ford of the Mary Ford Cake Artistry Centre, Mary Ford Books, Emerson Court, Alderley Road, Wilmslow, Cheshire, SK9 1NX; 01625 535353

You should also be able to find many other books on cakes, cake decoration and cake design at your local library.

Way 12 Calligraphy

Calligraphy is the art of handwriting. It requires skill, practice and the right tools, but once acquired it lends itself to many applications and could form the basis of a very successful business.

Calligraphy in the form of verses, quotes, names and initials can be applied to a wide range of different craft items such as calendars, greeting cards and bookmarks, leading the way into the lucrative gift market. Sell them direct to the public on your own market stall, or wholesale them to gift shops.

Businesses also provide exciting opportunities: museums, shops, estate agents, churches, clubs, societies, antique dealers, restaurants and hotels all use either display cards, invitation cards, dinner place cards, menus or posters. And what about other alphabets such as Greek, Russian and Hebrew? Perhaps this could form the basis of a specialism for you. And think about contacting your local printers. They could earn themselves a commission by passing on valuable customers to you – and vice versa.

Keep your eyes open for shops and businesses whose notices and displays you could improve. Price the work beforehand and then approach them in person, showing examples of the sort of work you do. Contact other businesses that you wish to target.

Calligraphy has a multitude of applications just waiting to be explored. If you can offer a quick, efficient service with this skill, it could prove to be your opening into the world of self-employment.

This will appeal if

- You have an obvious ability in this field.
- You're creative.
- You're happy doing repetitive work.

Advantages

- Reasonably low start-up costs, although if you intend to enter the gift market you will have some outlay on stock.
- There is a premium on hand-crafted work.
- It has lots of applications and therefore a potentially huge market to explore.

Disadvantages

- It can be repetitive (100 cards with the same greeting by Tuesday lunchtime?)
- Earnings are limited by your production capacity.

Future possibilities

- Use outworkers to increase production, eg art college students.
- Expand the range of craft items.
- Go into mass production – printing instead of individually handworking each item.
- Produce a range of 'How to …' videos on each writing style.

Address

Society of Scribes and Illuminators, 6 Queen Square, London WC1N 3AR; 01483 894155

Publications

Scribe. The magazine of the Society of Scribes and Illuminators.
Calligraphy Made Easy, Margaret Shepherd; Thorsons, 1996

There are numerous books now available on calligraphy. Ask your library for a current list.

Way 13 Car care

Petrol stations soon realised two facts: cars get dirty, and owners either don't like cleaning them, or don't have the time. They began to install car-wash machines. But for the busy executive, how much more convenient if the car wash could go to them.

This is where you come in, with a car-care service.

The benefits to customers are almost as important as the service itself. You will be saving their time and money (spent on petrol, driving around trying to find a car wash without a queue) and you will be selling convenience. You could include interior cleaning and car checks: water levels, engine oil and tyre pressures.

So think about how to find those customers. Remember that time is money and if you have to spend it travelling from one area to another this will cut down the amount of paying work you're able to do. Perhaps concentrate on one area to start with. Mail businesses direct, following up with a phone call. Aim to establish work on a contract basis which will ensure a steady work and cash flow.

You will be dealing with professional people and offering a

professional service; you too should look professional. Invest in a simple uniform – an overall printed with your business name will not only look good but also advertise your service to other potential customers.

Car care can be physically demanding, but the benefits you are able to offer, backed up by a first-class service, should form the basis for a very successful business.

This will appeal if

- You're reasonably fit.
- You enjoy manual work.
- You're reliable.
- You're happy working outdoors.
- You have a basic knowledge of cars if you intend to offer car-check services.

Advantages

- There is a perceived gap in the market for this service (do your own market research though).
- Good potential market.
- Good cash flow set-up.
- Low cost start-up.
- Low overheads.

Disadvantages

- Some work will be outdoors.
- Not much variety.
- Can be physically demanding.

Future possibilities

- Include a mobile car repair service.
- Increase profitability by buying service goods in bulk.
- Extend the area you cover by employing others.
- Expand into a nationwide network.
- Consider franchising the operation.
- Acquire premises to offer machine car-wash facilities.
- Market your own range of cleaning materials.

Address

British Car Wash Association, c/o Oakstead Holdings Ltd, The Pinnacles, Elizabeth Way, Harlow, Essex CM19 5AR; 01279 443221

Way 14 Card mailing service

Every year businesses spend small fortunes mailing Christmas cards and other literature to their customers and suppliers. Invariably it takes up someone's valuable time to organise and administer it – normally a secretary who already has plenty to do.

This is where you could help with a business which offers to handle such mailings from start to finish. You're selling convenience, organisation and efficiency to them with the added benefit of freeing staff to concentrate on their normal workload.

You could offer to buy in cards to sign and address on behalf of your client; have cards specially printed with the business's own wording; commission designs for individual companies. But apart from the Christmas rush, you could also remind customers of other mailings you could do for them: special offers, new products, business news updates, other PR activities, and card mailings for other religious festivals like Chinese New Year, Passover or the Muslim Eid festival. In this way you can ensure a more continuous work flow throughout the rest of the year.

Mail potential customers direct and think carefully about when to start this business if you want to key in to the Christmas period instantly. Two weeks before 25 December would be catastrophic!

If you're organised and think you could offer a highly efficient, top quality service to the business sector, card mailing could be the business for you.

This will appeal if

- You're organised.
- You're efficient.
- You're happy doing repetitive work.
- You enjoy clerical, desk-based work.

Advantages

- A simple business to operate once set up.

- Low cost start-up.
- It has lots of benefits to help sell the service.

Disadvantages

- Seasonal work unless you exploit other mailing opportunities.
- Not much variety.
- Ideally you need to invest in a computer.

Future possibilities

- Invest in a computer, if you haven't already.
- Acquire premises and install plant to mechanise procedures.
- Extend the services you offer to include PR work – buy in the skills if necessary, perhaps through freelances.
- Offer an international service with cards in other languages. Think about festivals in other countries: American Independence, Mardi Gras and even German unification!

Way 15 Careers advisor

The success of a business often depends on timing and being able to ride the wave of up and coming new trends. With recent changes in the job market, one such trend is for people to start thinking about their careers in a new light – especially when job security appears to be a thing of the past for many. Reassessing one's career is difficult to do alone, especially if a complete change of direction is needed. This is where the careers advisor comes in; and this is where your business opportunity starts.

Although Careers Offices are now starting to open their doors to adults, not everyone wants to proceed down that publicly-funded route, preferring instead to take private career counselling. This should tell you something about the likely clients for the service you offer. They are less likely to be school and/or college leavers, and more likely to be professionals in mid-career. This knowledge will affect how and where you advertise your services.

A background in psychology, recruitment and counselling are all highly relevant to setting up in this business. Understanding people, being able to assess accurately their strengths and weaknesses, having a working knowledge of the job market, and being able to help people navigate their way through what may be a difficult process are all necessary skills for success in career counselling.

Helping people make a decision about their next career move may be the limit of the service you decide to offer. On the other hand, you might want to offer in addition to basic career counselling CV preparation, training in interview techniques and other related job-hunting skills, to provide a more comprehensive service to clients in their search for a successful career.

This will appeal if

- You enjoy meeting people and have good interpersonal skills.
- You are able to give objective advice.
- You are organised.
- You have an analytical mind.

Advantages

- Low cost start-up.
- Low overheads – depending on office location.
- Can be run from home, visiting clients where they live.
- You would be providing a worthwhile service.

Disadvantages

- Little repeat business.
- May be a difficult business to sustain in less densely populated areas.
- On-going advertising costs.
- Competition from publicly-funded services.

Future possibilities

- Build up a staff with sector specialisms.
- Provide a countrywide network.
- Franchise the operation.
- Provide an Internet-based service.
- Produce a video for job-hunters and career-changers.
- Tender for government contracts to provide a local careers service.

Address

Institute of Personnel and Development, IPD House, Camp Road, London SW19 4UX; 0181-971 9000.

Publications
The IPD Code of Practice for Career and Outplacement Consultants (address above)
The Careers Adviser's Guide, Rebecca Corfield; Kogan Page, 1995

Way 16 Catering service

Think about how many times food is eaten in a domestic or business/office setting on special occasions, both formal and informal: birthday celebrations, Christmas parties, lengthy in-house meetings, working lunches and product launches, to name a few. The regularity of these 'eat-ins' presents you with an excellent opportunity to build a business which services these needs.

Consider the selection you could offer, ranging from basic or fancy sandwiches to more 'executive' fork food provision or full sit down meals. You could also offer a waitress service, a wine service, a specialist vegetarian selection, and even an organic one too.

Mail customers direct with leaflets to explain about and advertise your service. You could even deliver some free sandwiches to businesses to launch the venture, leaving cards and leaflets with the food as well as napkins and plates printed with your business name and address. People need to know who you are and how to find you.

Pay attention to looking clean and hygienic. Think about a simple uniform to help reinforce that image. You will also need to apply for a food-handling license from your local Environmental Health Officer.

This will appeal if

- You have some basic culinary skills.
- You're happy doing repetitive work – five dozen cheese and relish sandwiches in one go?
- You're organised and reliable.
- You have good food presentation skills.

Advantages

- Potentially huge market.
- Good mark-up on finger foods.
- Low investment in stock – you buy supplies as you need them.
- Good cash flow set-up.

Disadvantages

- You need space for hygienic storage and handling of food.
- You need transport.
- Could take some time to become established.

Future possibilities

- Expand into catering on a larger scale, eg functions and conferences.
- Expand into neighbouring towns.
- Develop the drinks service.

Addresses

Cookery and Food Association, 1 Victoria Parade, by 331 Sandycombe Road, Richmond, Surrey TW9 3NB; 0181-948 3870

European Catering Association, Bourne House, Horsell Park, Woking, Surrey GU21 4LY; 01483 750991

Hotel, Catering and International Management Association, 191 Trinity Road, London SW17 7HN; 0181-672 4251

British Hospitality Association, 40 Duke Street, London W1M 6HR; 0171-404 7744

Publications
Catering and Hospitality News (quarterly)
Running Your Own Catering Company, Judy Ridgway, 2nd edition; Kogan Page, 1992

Way 17 Children's party entertainer

Entertaining children can be an incredibly enjoyable way to start your own business. Children love to be entertained and you can help to take the strain off parents whose energies may have already been spent on simply organising the event.

Decide what sort of character you're going to be. If necessary watch some children's programmes to get some ideas. The age of the children will affect your choice. Games, prizes, style of presentation, length of presentation, type of jokes and songs will all be affected by their age as well. The amount of space and location (indoors or out) will also be important. Have a number of different repertoires to hand.

This sort of business will respond well to regular advertising in local papers. You could also advertise with posters or leaflets in cake shops, toy shops and newsagents.

Prices should be carefully worked out. Be precise about what your programme offers and the amount of time you will spend at each venue. Include the cost of balloons, paper hats, streamers and prizes – with your name and address on as many as possible.

Once your reputation is established your work should be its own advertisement. Then you could soon find yourself with a regular supply of work and the prospect of being a sure-fire business success.

This will appeal if

- You enjoy working with children.
- You have some understanding of their needs at different ages.
- You enjoy performing.
- You have lots of energy – children can be very demanding.
- You have lots of imagination.

Advantages

- Low cost start-up.
- Good cash flow set-up.
- Lots of fun.
- Your reputation becomes its own advertisement.

Disadvantages

- Can be repetitive – but then you can always change your act.
- It's physically demanding.

- You could be a huge flop with some children – which is why you need different repertoires and to be very imaginative.
- Work will be intermittent at first.

Future possibilities

- Playing to larger audiences, eg at hotels or children's clubs and societies.
- With a full schedule you could hire others to facilitate expansion.
- Expand the geographical area you cover.
- Develop an entertainments booking agency to cover adult entertainment too.
- Produce and sell videos of your performances.
- Write books about how to entertain children.

Publications

Children's parties, Juliet Moxley; Ebury Press, 1993
Successful Children's Parties, Julia Goodwin; Merehurst, 1995
Entertaining Children, Janell Shride Amos; McFarland & Co, 1993

Way 18 Cleaning antiques

There are lots of books around to help set yourself up in this business. Combine your knowledge with a good dash of common sense and you could soon have a flourishing trade.

Specialising applies well to this business: porcelain, pottery, jewellery, glassware, furniture, silver, light fittings, dolls. (Not paintings, please. This requires highly specialised skills. Very old fabrics are the same.) Have a good brainstorming session, decide on one or two areas in which to concentrate and begin to develop your expertise. Practise on junk items at first. Learn all you have to *before* you attempt to scour your first customer's beautiful antique enamelled clock face!

Market research should show you how big the potential market is in your area. If all looks well, regular advertising in your local papers should start to get you known and bring in custom. Once you are established you could think about approaching small museums, stately homes, hotels, restaurants, churches and antique shops. And keep your business cards with you in case you spot a potential customer while you're out and about.

Always be clear about the limits of your service because repair and renovation work is another ball game entirely. If in doubt about whether you can do the work, decline. In this case it might be worth forming links with a restorer who could do the work, while you take a commission instead.

Also, be careful about the pricing of your work. People are paying not only for your time but also for your expertise. Too cheap and they may become suspicious, too expensive and they may have second thoughts.

This will appeal if

- You have some knowledge about cleaning antiques.
- You're good at working with your hands.
- You're a careful worker with an eye for detail.

Advantages

- You could start in your spare time.
- Low overheads.
- It could lead to regular contracts: 'Clean my silver once a month.'
- Lots of variety.

Disadvantages

- Possibility of damages or breakages – find out about insurance.
- Could take time to build up a regular work flow.
- Earnings are limited by the number of hours in a day.

Future possibilities

- Build a team of people with different specialisms.
- With further training, or by buying in the skills, move into renovation work.
- Begin dealing in antiques.
- Acquire shop premises to sell cleaned and renovated antiques.

Publication
How to Restore and Repair Practically Everything, Lorraine Johnson, new edition; Michael Joseph, 1988

Way 19 Community business

If setting up and running a business holds a strong appeal, but raising the necessary funds to do so is a problem, establishing a community business could provide the answer.

Community businesses are commercially-run enterprises whose profits are ploughed back into the community to create new jobs or help fund other projects. So if your sole aim in running a business is to become a millionaire, this is not the route for you. If, however, you want to earn a decent living in a commercial environment with a socially-minded focus, this could be what you are looking for.

Almost any venture can be set up as a community business, providing it caters to the needs of an identified 'community' (ie any group of people sharing a common bond). Without being able to justify it in those terms it will be difficult, if not impossible, to raise the necessary funds. None of the start-up costs need come from your own pocket. Instead, community businesses are funded by grants from the government, national lottery, European Social Fund, corporate funders, local councils, and individual grant-making trusts.

To make a successful bid you need to demonstrate how the business would be answering the needs of the community, and that it could be run successfully along commercial lines. Those projects which clearly show they can become self-financing in due course are more likely to be favoured. All will be judged on how professionally they will be run and the credentials of those involved.

Cafes, nurseries, road weather forecasting, publishing, manufacturing, shops, and contract cleaning are among the wide range of community businesses which have been successfully set up throughout the country. Get together with some like-minded others and see what ideas you can come up with for a community business for your area.

This will appeal if

- You want to help improve your local area.
- You have management or other skills to bring to the business.
- You have a good understanding of your 'community'.
- You enjoy working collaboratively.
- Fat-cat salaries are less important to you than doing a worthwhile job.

Advantages

- You do not have to have money of your own to set up an enterprise.
- You will be making a positive contribution towards alleviating social and/or economic pressures.
- Provides an opportunity to create your own paid employment and make use of existing skills.

Disadvantages

- Profits are ploughed back into the community – not into your own pocket.
- Fund-raising can be time-consuming.
- Driving a community business forward can be demanding.

Future possibilities

- These largely depend on the community which is being served by the business and how much profit is generated by the enterprise. Either the business itself could expand to create more jobs or generate finance to fund new projects.

Address

Community Development Foundation, 60 Highbury Grove, London N5 2AG; 0171-226 5375

Publication
Directory of Grant-making Trusts, Charities Aid Foundation. Available in most libraries.

Way 20 Companions agency

Many people from all walks of life would like a companion – not someone to date or a marriage partner, but just someone else to be there. The elderly and disabled are two groups which come to mind, but what about people wanting travel or holiday companions, someone to go on regular outings with or to accompany them to a special function? Some are geographically isolated or isolated through bereavement. The potential market appears to be huge.

Market research your area. You may find a demand in only one or two of the above categories but once you have decided that the demand is good enough, recruit your companions. Do it carefully, asking for full references. And it could be a good idea to run them through a training programme on the dos and don'ts of their work.

Advertising needs to be carefully thought out. Local newspapers are fine, but watch how you word the ads; you don't want to give the impression that you're running an escort agency which has different connotations. Church magazines and doctors' surgeries could be good places to advertise, adding an additional air of respectability to your operation.

With little more than a telephone, some printed stationery and a bookings diary, setting up a companions agency could provide a much needed service.

This will appeal if

- You have excellent interpersonal skills.
- You're reliable, organised and efficient.
- You're good at managing staff.
- You're good at understanding people's needs.

Advantages

- Low cost start-up.
- You can start up on your own.
- A regular income once your customer base is established.
- Earning potential high since there is no limit to the number of clients you take on.

Disadvantages

- May take time to become established.
- May find it difficult to recruit the right staff.
- Office space isn't essential to start but would help later as you expand.

Future possibilities

- Establish operations in other towns/cities.
- Expand the agency work into other areas: escorting children to and from boarding school, nannies, dating, catering staff, temping etc.
- Acquire premises and establish a social club.

Way 21 Complementary therapies

More and more people are starting to question orthodox medicine and complementary therapies are coming into their own. This presents a wide range of exciting opportunities for you – as a complementary therapist.

There are a vast number of different areas in which to work: homoeopathy, herbalism, colour therapy, rebirthing, crystal therapy, massage and aromatherapy, to name a few. But whichever you decide upon, you will need to be professionally trained. The Institute for Complementary Therapies will supply you with a list of bona fide organisations which offer training courses, some of which also look at how to set up and run a practice.

The great advantage of this business, besides it being in a growth area, is that both the training and the practice itself can normally be fitted into your spare time; evenings and weekends are when most of your patients will want to see you. It gives you the opportunity to build your customer base gradually and establish your practice.

Although initially offering one therapy, you could train in others later on. In fact, it would help to widen your potential customer base – each therapy has its own limitations.

Advertise your services in local health food shops, 'alternative' health magazines and even your local paper. But once your reputation becomes established you may find your work becomes its own advertisement.

This will appeal if

- You're interested in health.
- You have a genuine desire to help people.
- You have an analytical mind.
- You have good interpersonal skills.

Advantages

- It's an expanding market.
- Low overheads, depending on which therapy and how you operate – visiting people or running your practice from your own home will obviously be cheaper than acquiring premises.
- You can start in your spare time.

Disadvantages

- Can be demanding.
- May take some time to become established.
- Can be repetitive, depending on the therapy.

Future possibilities

- Extend the range of therapies in which you are proficient.
- Establish a joint practice with other therapists.
- Open other practices around the country.
- Run training courses.
- Depending on the therapy, develop your own commercial product range.

Address

Institute for Complementary Medicine, PO Box 194, London SE16 1QZ; 0171-237 5165. Send an SAE and 2 stamps.

Way 22 Contract cleaning

Let's be honest. Few people would say they want to set up this business because of a love of the work itself. But if you're handy with a hoover or dapper with a duster, you could have a budding business at your fingertips. Potential customers for commercial premises include shops, offices and banks. Customers for home valeting might include single parents; busy executives; people who have just moved house, held a party or had builders in; and landlords with property to let.

You may only want to offer a vacuum and dusting service, but you could offer washing-up, bathroom cleaning, window washing and floor mopping. Special services could include things like spring cleaning or patio brush-ups.

Find customers through leaflet drops and advertising in local papers or newsagents' windows. Contact landlords (through accommodation agencies) and builders – who could improve the quality of their own services by using yours. For commercial customers approach businesses direct.

You may intend to keep the business small but you should still do some market research. Find out what people expect from their cleaning service. Are they getting it at present? If not, could you provide what they want? Use your market research to find out about the local going rate to help you work out your costs. Remember you can compete on things other than price: quality of service and reliability are excellent selling points. Think also about image. A smart, simple uniform gets you away from the Mrs Mop idea and reinforces the quality aspect of the very valuable service your business provides.

This will appeal if

- You're reasonably fit.
- You're reliable.
- You enjoy routine.

Advantages

- Steady workflow and income once customer base is established.
- It's a job with few work pressures.
- Can be a very low cost start-up.

Disadvantages

- It isn't exactly glamorous work.
- Initially, earnings are limited by the number of hours you can work.
- Not much variety.
- Relatively low pay.

Future possibilities

- Recruit additional staff to respond to increased workload.
- Expand into other maintenance work: window cleaning (Way 99), curtain making, upholstery service, security work (Way 84).
- Tender for larger cleaning contracts.
- Expand into other geographical areas.
- Franchise the operation.
- Market your own brand of cleaning materials.

Addresses

Cleaning and Support Services Association, Suite 73/74, The Hop Exchange, 24 Southwark Street, London SE1 1TY; 0171-403 2747

Cleaning and Hygiene Suppliers Association, 246–254 High Street, Sutton, Surrey SM1 1PA; 0181-643 0689

Publication
Cleaning and Hygiene Today (monthly)

Way 23 Counselling

Communities are much less stable than they used to be. Support structures are harder to find even though people may have a greater need for them, trying to cope with life's incessant demands.

When a problem arises not everyone has access to supportive friends or relatives. Others would rather not share problems with those they know. If you have a talent for helping others sort out their lives, you could turn it into paying work and a way into self-employment.

At present you need no special qualifications or licences to set up a counselling service. But although you may be naturally gifted in this field, training would be a good idea. There's a difference between telling someone what to do and helping them reach the right decision by themselves.

Problems which people may bring to you could range from stress and bereavement to money problems and life crises. You could decide to specialise in one particular area. For example, if your experience has been in the business world you could counsel people in business. Phone around and find out what the going rate is.

Rent a small office, preferably with a waiting room, or if your home is suitable you could even start off from there. Advertise in your local paper, church magazines or a specialist magazine if you decide to target your work. Health food shops and 'alternative' magazines could also be worth investigating. Before long you could be running a very successful business, one of the few which benefits people directly in a very real sense.

This will appeal if

- You have good interpersonal skills.
- You have an analytical mind.
- You have a common-sense approach to life.
- You're non-judgemental.
- You have the ability to be objective yet still empathise.

Advantages

- Low cost start-up.
- Potentially large market, especially if you're in or near a city.
- You're offering a valuable service to people.
- You can take on as many or as few clients as you want.

Disadvantages

- Training is advisable.
- The work can be emotionally demanding.

Future possibilities

- Establish a practice which brings in others with different counselling skills to complement those which you offer.
- Give talks.
- Run training courses.

Address

British Association for Counselling, 1 Regent Place, Rugby, Warwicks CV21 2PJ; 01788 578328

Publications
Careers in Counselling, Myra Bennett and the British Association for Counselling, revised edition; BAC, 1990
Counselling (quarterly), BAC

Way 24 Courier services

Fast communication is a must for businesses but despite the proliferation of fax machines, mobile phones and the Internet, there are still some items which need to be delivered by hand – immediately. A courier service fulfils that very real need.

Photographs, legal documents, plans and drawings, computer disks, artwork and medical items are some of the things which need same day, even instant, delivery. Looking at this list, think about who your potential clients are. You may decide to specialise and target one particular group. This is a good idea, making it easier to market yourself. Simply mail identified businesses direct and include a business card/leaflet/sticker.

But do your market research first. Find out which groups are interested and what they want from a service – something which perhaps others are not providing: an overnight service, long-distance work, politeness, or bike riders who remove their intimidating helmets when they call. Find out what they want.

The type of work you do will decide the transport you need – or vice versa. Cars are good for larger parcels and long journeys; bicycles are excellent for smaller documents and cutting through tiresome traffic.

You might like to think about a simple uniform, too. Remember that while you're out on the road you can be advertising your business. Have your jacket, vehicle and/or bags boldly printed with your business name and mobile telephone number.

It may take time to become established, but if you can provide an efficient and reliable service, the repeat business you receive should ensure your business success.

This will appeal if

- You enjoy driving/cycling.
- You enjoy working on your own.

- You're a good time-keeper.
- You're reliable.

Advantages

- You're not confined to an office.
- Varied work.
- Low cost start-up, assuming you already have some form of transport.

Disadvantages

- You do need some form of transport to start.
- Earnings are limited by the number of calls you can make in a day.
- Can be tiring work, driving all day.
- It's all-weather work – important if you're a bike courier.

Future possibilities

- Hire premises and install someone to take bookings.
- Build a team of couriers to enable you to cover wider areas.
- Establish branches around the country.
- Franchise the operation.
- Compete for international work.

Address

Despatch Association, 7 Lavington Street, London SE1 0NZ; 0171-620 0775

Publication
Courier Express (bi-monthly)

Way 25 Craftwork

Establishing a business based on craftwork gives you the opportunity to turn your favourite hobby or special skills into paying work.

Genuine handicrafts are always popular amid today's mass produced items. The more original and novel your designs, the better. But do some thorough market research. Take your samples around likely shops. You may find that packaging is important to buyers, who may suggest including information about production methods and materials you use, which should also be environmentally friendly.

Assess their reactions to your proposed prices. From this you can work out whether the market would support your work. Be realistic in your assessment. Although you love making your brightly coloured whatnots, if it costs you £5 to make one and the shops would only buy at £3, think again!

But if the reactions are positive, and you can make them for the right price, there are lots of sales opportunities: craft shops, gift shops, by mail order, through a party plan arrangement, on a market stall or at craft fairs.

This will appeal if

- You have a craft skill.
- You have some basic selling skills, or are willing to acquire them.
- You can maintain standards of production.

Advantages

- People always need to buy gifts.
- You can tailor designs to suit customers' needs, and to reflect market trends.
- It's an enjoyable way to be self-employed.
- You can start off in your spare time.

Disadvantages

- It can be monotonous making 50 orange whatnots every day.
- Investment in stock needed.
- It can be difficult balancing production time with selling.
- Requires a workspace.

Future possibilities

- Find an agent to do the selling for you.
- Depending on the type of work, use outworkers.
- Form a co-operative with other craftworkers.

- Acquire shop premises and sell complementary products.
- Export.

Addresses

Guild of Master Craftsmen, 166 High Street, Lewes, East Sussex BN7 1XU; 01273 478449

Crafts Council, 44a Pentonville Road, London N1 9BY; 0171-278 7700

Publications
Crafts (bi-monthly) Crafts Council
The Craftsman Magazine (bi-monthly)
The Craftworker's Year Book (bi-annual)

Way 26 Cultivating new plants

Avid gardeners will be well aware that new strains of plants are continuously finding their way onto the market. Although many are developed by the large commercial seed companies, there is always room for a new plant variety which successfully catches the gardening public's eye. It matters not whether it is developed by the commercial company themselves or by a keen gardener in their part-time.

When you have developed what you think is a new cultivar, contact the national collection holder of that particular species. It is important to establish that what you have growing in your greenhouse is new, or whether it is one which already exists. If it is a new one, registration of the plant by its new name is the next important step. There are international guidelines established to help you do this (see below).

Entering into an agreement with a commercial seed company should typically yield an on-going income of 10 per cent of commercial sales. In exchange they will test, package and market the seeds and/or plants to the general public. Signing a trialing contract while they test the plant is important to make sure you remain the owner of all material derived from the plant itself while it is under trial.

Without direct access to the market it would be difficult

(though not impossible) and costly to handle the production and distribution by yourself. It also means that by allowing someone else to handle the commercial aspect you are then free to concentrate on developing other new strains.

Plant and seed sales are big business, especially in the UK, though it has to be said that as with any new product it is the minority which make the really big bucks. But if you have especially gifted green fingers you could find that cultivating new plants brings you a lucrative share in this vast market.

This will appeal if

- You have a specialist knowledge of particular plant breeds.
- You enjoy experimenting.
- You are methodical in keeping notes of your 'experiments'.
- You have another source of income until your plants start generating sales.

Advantages

- Can be started part-time or be a lucrative spin-off to an existing hobby.
- As a keen gardener already, there is unlikely to be much in the way of additional start-up costs.
- Once on the retail market, income generates itself with no further work from you.
- Additional income from each new plant strain developed.

Disadvantages

- The majority of 'new' plants don't make it past the trialing stage.
- Is a long process – there's no way to rush nature while you develop a new strain and have it trialed.
- Need another source of income until plants get past the trialing stage.

Future possibilities

- Continue developing new strains.
- Expand and become a commercial propagator.

- Publish books/videos, using your specialist knowledge.
- Run courses, give lectures.

Addresses

Hardy Plants Society, Little Orchard, Great Comberton, Near Pershore, Worcestershire WR10 3DP; 01386 710317

Royal Horticultural Society, Wisley, Woking, Surrey GU23 6QB; 01483 224234

Publication
International Code of Nomenclature of Cultivated Plants. Available from the Royal Horticultural Society.

Way 27 Dealing in art

On visiting a local Art College show, I was surprised by how much talent was there and thought about the potential opportunity just waiting to be realised by someone. Could it be you?

Dealing in new artists' work enables you to set up a business without having to invest in stock. You agree to try to sell work, and in exchange you take a commission – normally about 40 per cent. Prices are negotiated with each artist, not only to cover your overheads, but also to put a realistic premium on their work.

Although you don't have to buy stock, you must have display space – your own living room if it is stylish enough to enhance displays, and has good lighting. Alternatively, rent space in suitable shops, cafés or bars. The best way is to acquire premises.

To be successful you must be good at PR. Get yourself and your gallery known. Advertise in art magazines and local papers. Send press releases to people who could either promote each exhibition or be potential buyers. And while collectors may be the mainstay of your business, think also about interior designers and other art 'users'.

How many pieces you sell ultimately depends on your choice of work. But you can help the selling process along. Make sure you look after potential buyers; have fresh coffee or wine to offer them. And who knows, it might be just the thing to tip another successful sale in your favour.

This will appeal if

- You know something about art.
- You have a good eye for spotting talented work.
- You're good at PR.
- You have good interpersonal skills.
- You have some selling skills – or are willing to pick up the basics.

Advantages

- Very good profit margins.
- No investment in stock needed.
- Good cash flow set-up.
- The selling becomes easier once your reputation is established.

Disadvantages

- Overheads of premises.
- Your idea of good art might not be anyone else's (apart from the artist's).
- The art market is easily affected by economic downturns.

Future possibilities

- Acquire premises in other cities.
- Acquire premises abroad.
- Offer prints/modern reproductions.
- Begin to deal in work other than by new artists.
- Trade up-market.

Address

Society of London Art Dealers, 91 Jermyn Street, London SW1Y 6JB; 0171-930 6137

Publications
Artists Newsletter (monthly)
Galleries
Art Review Yearbook

Way 28 Driving tuition

Each year sees a new group of 18-year-olds emerge wanting to learn how to drive. With additional training you could use your existing skills, help these youngsters learn, and find yourself running a successful business.

But before you go ahead, do your market research. Find out how much competition there is. Could you take a big enough market share to support your business? What's the going rate, and could you improve on the service which existing driving schools offer?

If the prospects look good, apply to the Driving Standards Agency for their starter pack – it is essential reading. In it you will find details about the three exams you will have to pass (written, driving and instructional) before getting your Approved Driving Instructor's licence. It could take up to six months or longer, depending on how competent you are. Use the extra time to plan your advertising campaign, sort out fine details and perhaps arrange for your car to have dual controls fitted.

Advertise in local papers and Yellow Pages. Think about targeting particular groups: young learners, motorway drivers or caravan owners. Give talks to local groups like the Women's Institute. But once your reputation becomes established you will find that you are your own best advertisement in helping to ensure that your business succeeds.

This will appeal if

- You enjoy driving.
- You have good interpersonal skills.
- You're calm and patient.

Advantages

- Good cash flow set-up.
- Presents an opportunity to capitalise on skills and assets.
- A lot of work comes through personal recommendation.
- Personal satisfaction when learners pass.

Disadvantages

- Needs qualifications.

- You need to own or have access to a car – possibly with dual controls.
- Earnings are limited by the number of hours you work.
- Evening and weekend work is involved.

Future possibilities

- Acquire new vehicles and recruit other instructors.
- Acquire premises from which to operate.
- Invest in simulated driving equipment.
- Establish branches in other towns.
- Like BSM, franchise the operation.

Addresses

Driving Standards Agency, Stanley House, Talbot Street, Nottingham, NG1 5GU; 0115 955 7600 for details of starter pack which is also compulsory reading.

Register of Approved Driving Instructors, Department of Transport, Room C193, 2 Marsham Street, London SW1P 3EB; 0171-276 3000

He-Man Equipment Ltd, 23–27 Princes Street, Northam, Southampton SO1 1RP; 01703 226952. Supply dual-control equipment and will advise of garages which fit it.

Driving Instructor's Association, Safety House, Beddington Farm Road, Croydon CR0 4XZ; 0181-665 5151

Publications

The Driving Instructor's Handbook, John Miller and Margaret Stacey; Kogan Page, 1996 (recommended by the Department of Transport)

Driving Magazine (bi-monthly)

Way 29 Film making

A whole range of film-making exists which embraces more than just the feature length productions seen at the cinema. Although this may be the aim of many who enter the profession, other avenues offer scope within film production. This includes making corporate videos, training videos, television drama, pop videos, television documentaries and animation. Many top directors have started their careers making television commercials.

Although film training is available, this is still one profession in which people can start at the bottom and work up. Directors need some background knowledge in order to appreciate the technical limitations of the medium in which they are working, and to be able to communicate effectively with their colleagues on set so that the desired result is achieved. Producers, on the other hand, need sound judgement to be able to decide which ideas would translate into successful films, have the necessary contacts with backers who would fund the project, and have first rate organisational skills to be able to carry the project forward and within budget.

Having good ideas for films is not enough in this business – the right contacts are vital, too. Would-be independent directors and producers network their way into projects, especially at the features end of the spectrum.

Corporate and other training videos depend less on who you know but need good marketing to win the top contracts. Highly sophisticated, computer-generated special effects are now used in many of these commercial productions. The competition is equally tough in this specialised field, but if you can convince the right people of your ability to make a film to suit their needs, budget and commercial or other aims, you could find yourself making your first tentative steps towards Hollywood.

This will appeal if

- You have a background in the industry or are prepared to work your way into it.
- You can cope with high levels of stress.
- You have excellent interpersonal and communication skills.
- You are good at self-promotion – this is no business for the shrinking violet.
- You enjoy multi-task work.

Advantages

- Working in a creative field.

- Working in films still carries lots of kudos.
- The potential earnings are high.
- You are risking other people's money, not your own.

Disadvantages

- Getting your first break may take some time.
- Gaps between projects can make for a difficult cash flow.
- A stressful occupation – which may or may not be to your liking.
- Reputations can be easily ruined – producing a single 'flop' can be disastrous to your career.

Future possibilities

- Depends at which level you enter and what your personal aims and ambitions are. Some may be happy producing pop videos ad infinitum, while others use it merely as a launch-pad for their career: Hollywood or bust.

Addresses

Directors Guild of Great Britain, 15–19 Great Titchfield Street, London W1P 7FB; 0171-436 8626

Advertising Film and Videotape Producers Association, 26 Noel Street, London W1V 3RD; 0171-434 2651

British Film Institute, 21 Stephen Street, London W1P 2LN; 0171-255 1444

New Producers Alliance, 9 Bourlet Close, London W1P 7PJ; 0171-580 2480

Producers Alliance for Cinema and Television (PACT), 45 Mortimer Street, London W1N 7TD; 0171-331 6000

Publications

Film & TV Yearbook, British Film Institute

How to Get Into Films and TV, Robert Angell, 3rd edition; How to Books Ltd, 1996

Kemps International Film, TV and Video Yearbook.

Broadcast (weekly)

Business Video (weekly)
Screen Finance (fortnightly)
Screen International (weekly)
Sight and Sound (monthly)

Way 30 Florist's commission work

Supplying flowers and floral displays to businesses is the basis of this work, although it does not involve you in making any displays yourself. Instead, you enter into agreements with florists to whom you pass on orders, in exchange for a 10–20 per cent commission – not only for the initial order but for the duration of the contract.

Just think of all the businesses which use flowers: hotels, restaurants, coffee bars; in fact, any business which deals directly with the public – banks, solicitors, showrooms. The list is endless once you start to brainstorm.

So, first of all, have two contracts professionally drawn up: one for you and the florist, and one for you and your customer. Then approach a florist, finalise your agreement, work out your prices, and take photographs of sample displays to show potential customers.

You will be approaching businesses direct, either by mail or in person. Remember to sell the benefits: everything from cheering their customers to helping to humanise the environment (especially important in doctors' and dentists' waiting rooms).

Basically this is a selling job and to be successful you need to be enthusiastic about the product and able to communicate your enthusiasm to your clients.

This will appeal if

- You're good at, and enjoy, selling.
- You're enthusiastic about flowers and plants.
- You have an 'eye' for interior decor – you will need to be able to suggest which type of display would suit best.

Advantages

- No investment needed.
- Once the account is established the income generates itself.

- Excellent opportunities in a potentially huge market.
- Earnings are not limited by the number of hours you can work.

Disadvantages

- Ideally you need a car.
- Selling doesn't suit everyone.
- A drop in standards from your florist will reflect on your business.

Future possibilities

- Almost limitless in terms of business turnover.
- Wholesale flowers yourself instead of handing over contracts to other florists.
- Acquire shop premises and install a manager to take advantage of passing trade.

Addresses

British Retail Florists' Association, 60 Glebe Road, Loughor, Swansea SA4 6QD; 01792 892629

Flowers and Plants Association, Covent House, New Covent Garden Market, London SW8 5NX; 0171-738 8044

Publications
The Florist (monthly)
Complete Florist (monthly)

Way 31 Fortune telling

Whether you believe in fortune telling or not, it is very popular. Perhaps you can see your own fortune being made here?

There are many different methods: Tarot cards, playing cards, palm reading, I Ching, runes, astrology and others including the popular tea leaf reading. Training is available in some, like astrology, but most of them can be picked up through private study and lots of practice.

It is a business which you can easily start at home in your spare time, and as you become proficient you will soon find customers by word of mouth. But still advertise in local papers and/or specialist magazines. Find out beforehand what the going rate is for readings.

There are also numerous festivals and fairs where you could hire a stand. You could also consider operating at your local market (see Way 54). A prestigious London store has had its own resident fortune teller – could you negotiate such a deal?

You could also consider specialising in terms of a target market. One astrologer works with businesses, advising them on planetary influences which may affect the timing of plans and relationships within their organisation.

So, with lots of application, study and practice you could find that as we progress through the Aquarian age, so too does your fortune telling business.

This will appeal if

- You have good interpersonal skills.
- You have a good memory – there is a lot to learn in each fortune telling skill area.
- You are genuine.

Advantages

- Low cost start-up.
- Low overheads.
- Good cash flow set-up.
- If you're good, your reputation will soon grow.

Disadvantages

- Intermittent work to begin with.
- Can be exhausting when doing it full time.
- May need premises if you can't or don't want to work from home.
- Earnings are limited by the number of readings you can do in a day.

Future possibilities

- I'm tempted to say you'll be able to see for yourself!

- Extend your repertoire of fortune-telling skills.
- Acquire premises and sub-let spaces to others; advertise collectively under one name.
- Acquire shop premises from which to operate and sell related retail stock.

Publication
Prediction (monthly)

There are now numerous books available on a wide range of fortune-telling subjects. Consult your local bookshop or library.

Way 32 Franchising

Franchising is an interesting way into self-employment. You buy a tried and tested business blueprint, agree to pay an ongoing percentage fee of profits to the franchisor, and in exchange you receive: training, full back-up and support, advice, the right to use the franchise name, access to purchasing facilities as well as any secret recipes or formulas. You also receive the benefits of centrally organised advertising campaigns.

Franchises appear to increase the likelihood of business success but, before you dash straight into the first agreement you find, you still need to do your market research. Unfortunately, not all advertised franchises are bona fide. The British Franchise Association can help here. They produce a Franchise Information Pack which among other things includes a checklist for franchisees. Also, contact your bank and ask to see their franchise manager whose expertise in this field should be helpful.

Franchising is a cross between employment and self-employment. You are limited to some extent in the business decisions you can make because of franchise agreement restrictions, so you will not be as independent as a sole trader who sets up a business on his or her own. However, franchises do offer a more secure way in which to set out in the world of business. Is it for you?

This will appeal if

- You want a secure way into business.

- The training and ongoing support would be useful to you.
- Your independence is less important than getting into business and making it work.

Advantages

- You receive training, back-up and support.
- It's a less risky way into business.
- You need no prior knowledge.
- You receive the benefits of an established name and reputation.

Disadvantages

- Lack of full independence.
- Requires investment capital.
- You have an ongoing fee to pay.
- Your operation can be affected by the reputation of the franchisor and other franchisees.

Future possibilities

You may be restricted by your franchise agreement, but you could:

- Acquire more than one operation in the franchise.
- Acquire other types of franchises.
- Sell the franchise(s) and go solo.

Address

British Franchise Association, Thames View, Newtown Road, Henley-on-Thames, Oxon RG9 1HG; 01491 578049. Their Franchise Information Pack helps you to evaluate a franchise operation. Send for details.

Publications
The UK Franchise Directory (annual)
The Franchise Magazine (quarterly)
Franchise World (bi-monthly)
Taking Up a Franchise; The Daily Telegraph Guide, Colin Barrow and Godfrey Golzen; Kogan Page, annual
Business Franchise (monthly)

Way 33 Fundraising

Over recent years, the voluntary sector has grown enormously and become more professional in its operations. But because the sector has grown, so too has the competition for funds.

Large, well-established groups employ full-time fundraisers to generate an on-going inflow of monies. Smaller, less well-established groups do not necessarily have the finances available to employ anyone on even a part-time basis. These are the organisations who look to hire freelance fundraisers to help them in this vital area of work. Without adequate funds being raised, their chances of survival decline.

As with other 'consultants', work is charged on an hourly or daily rate, working to an agreed brief. Some fundraisers choose to limit their involvement to assessing a group's fundraising needs and advising them on their best strategy. Others prefer to be fully involved in the implementation of proposed fundraising activities. Decide which you would prefer.

Voluntary groups will want to know your credentials and be looking for reassurance that the cost of hiring a fundraiser will be money well-spent. They may also want to know your particular strengths or specialisms, like corporate giving, direct mail, sponsorships or launching appeals.

Organisations often find a fundraiser by word-of-mouth, or by contacting the Institute of Charity Fundraising Managers. Unless you already have particularly good contacts in the field you might also want to think about contacting direct those groups whose aims you particularly support or of which you have a working knowledge.

Becoming a professional fundraiser can be an excellent way of making your contribution to the voluntary sector a rewarding experience all round.

This will appeal if

- You like responsibility.
- You are organised and efficient.
- You enjoy working to targets.
- You have good interpersonal skills.
- You have a good understanding of the voluntary sector culture.

Advantages

- Can be lucrative.
- It's an expanding field.
- Low overheads – can even be run from home.

Disadvantages

- Competition for funds is tight – so you need to be sure you can deliver what you say and reach agreed targets.
- Working with the less efficiently-run voluntary groups can be frustrating.
- May find yourself working with a committee, which can often slow down the decision-making process.

Future possibilities

- Publish articles on the voluntary sector and your experience within it.
- Recruit other consultants, perhaps with specialisms to complement your own.
- Expand your area of expertise into, for example, recruitment.
- Develop a programme of conferences on fundraising.

Addresses

Institute of Charity Fundraising Managers, 208 Market Towers, 1 Nine Elms Lane, London SW8 5NQ; 0171-627 3436

National Council for Voluntary Organisations, Regents Wharf, 8 All Saints Street, London N1 9RL; 0171-713 6161

Publications
Professional Fundraising (monthly)
Practical Fundraising for Individuals and Small Groups, David Wragg; Piatkus, 1995
The Complete Fundraising Handbook; Directory of Social Change, 1993

Way 34 Garden work

A friend of mine pined for a garden for years. Now she has one she realises just how much looking after it takes and with a full-time job finds she has to hire garden help. She is like lots of others who need basic help in keeping their gardens tidy. If you enjoy this sort of work, it could form the basis of a good business venture for you.

Think about the services you could offer. You don't have to be a garden expert to do: garden clearance (be sure you agree on what needs pulling up and what doesn't), lawn mowing, hedge trimming, weeding, patio maintenance, leaf clearance, fencing, and so on. You could start by specialising in one service (for example, mowing lawns once a week) and build up from there. Do some market research in your area to find the likely take-up, most needed services, what the going rate is, and what the competition is like. Decide whether to charge by the hour or by the job and remember when you draw up your cash-flow statement that the winter months will affect the amount of paying work you can do.

You could advertise by leaflet drops to households as well as through local papers. You could also think about having a regular card in newsagents' windows and on local noticeboards, as well as advertising in local church magazines, too.

Investing in a simple uniform will help to reinforce your professional image: overalls, T-shirts or sweat shirts printed with your business name will do and won't cost you much. It's also a good way of advertising yourself and your work.

So if you're fit and a keen worker who enjoys working outdoors, you could try doing garden work.

This will appeal if

- You enjoy working outdoors.
- You like varied work.
- You're practical.
- You're physically fit.
- You're reliable.

Advantages

- Healthy work, giving you lots of exercise and fresh air.
- Excellent opportunities for repeat business.
- Good cash flow set-up.
- Can be varied.

Disadvantages

- Seasonal work, with the inevitable downturn in winter months.
- Must be physically fit.
- Some investment in equipment and transport an advantage.

Future possibilities

- Hire help to respond to increased workload.
- Acquire more gardening skills to be able to offer a greater range of services, or hire specialist help.
- Carry a range of garden supplies to sell.
- Establish operations in other areas.
- Franchise the operation.
- Open a garden shop/centre/nursery.

Way 35 Gift buying service

Buying gifts can be difficult – finding the time, thinking of something original, worrying if it's suitable. For busy executives, the house-bound or for businesses buying retirement, farewell or special award presents, this could be a service for which they would pay well.

Your job would be to find details about who the gift is for, the relationship between the giver and the receiver, how much is to be spent, as well as when and how the gift should be delivered (to the giver or receiver?). Have a list of suggestions to hand for both sexes and in different price ranges: edible/drinkable, romantic, practical, valedictory, for children, unusual, artistic, traditional and so on. You may decide to specialise in one particular type of gift; for example, champagne and roses or personalised crystal ware.

Your market need not necessarily be a local one so think about advertising in national magazines – ones which business executives and personnel managers read. Sunday and other national papers could also be possibilities. Or you may decide to mail executives direct at their business addresses (names and addresses in *Kompass Directory* at your local library.) Personnel managers could also be contacted direct. Your sales literature should reflect the up-market aspect of your business and what the service includes (gift selection, gift wrapping, delivery and any other unique features such as last minute deliveries) as well as stressing the benefits of such a service.

If this appeals to you, decide which gifts to include in your service; find your suppliers; negotiate special discounted rates – and off you go.

This will appeal if

- You're reliable.
- You're organised.
- You have a good understanding of people's needs.
- You have some advisory skills.

Advantages

- Can charge higher premiums to business clients.
- Repeat business a possibility.
- Low cost start-up.
- Low overheads.

Disadvantages

- Could take a while to become established.
- Seasonality – peaking at Christmas.

Future possibilities

- As your operation grows, larger discounts can be negotiated; you could even buy and stock items direct from manufacturers.
- Open branches in other towns/cities.
- Establish a mail order gift catalogue to distribute to households.

Publications
Gifts International (monthly)
Gifts Today (monthly)
Progressive Gifts (monthly)

Way 36 Grave care

Although the grounds of cemeteries and churchyards are regularly maintained, it is left up to surviving relatives and friends to look after the actual graves. As time goes by, many people may find themselves without the time, inclination or ability to make regular visits. A grave care service brings peace of mind to those who would rather know their friend's or relative's grave was being well looked after.

Decide what different types of service to offer: basic headstone cleaning; weeding; flower planting; delivery of cut flowers; visits once a week/month/six months/year. A thoughtful touch would be to send a snapshot of the grave so that your customers can see the work you have carried out.

Think about how to advertise. Church magazines and local papers could be a possibility. You could also negotiate with local undertakers to advertise your business in exchange for a commission, the benefit to them being that it appears to extend their own service. You could do the same with florists. But before you start, check with the churchyard or cemetery superintendent to make sure it is alright for you to work there.

Transport would be helpful and increase your efficiency but it is not essential; the tools you will be using will be basic and relatively lightweight. But there will be lots of bending down so you do need to be reasonably fit.

This is a valuable service to be offering to people and if you like outdoor work it could be for you.

This will appeal if

- You have some basic gardening ability, but regular gardening work doesn't appeal.
- You're conscientious.
- You enjoy working outdoors.
- You're reasonably fit.

Advantages

- It's quiet, peaceful work.

- Good cash flow set-up, getting customers to pay in advance when they place the order.
- Guaranteed work flow once customer base is established.
- Satisfying work.

Disadvantages

- Working outdoors.
- Earnings are limited by the number of hours you can work.
- Loss of earnings in winter because of shorter daylight hours and weather conditions.

Future possibilities

- Extend the range of services to include headstone replacement, newspaper In Memoriam inserts.
- Hire staff as workload increases.
- Establish operations in other areas.

Address

National Association of Funeral Directors, 618 Warwick Road, Solihull, West Midlands B91 1AA; 0121-711 1343

Way 37 Greeting card design

This business is for the artistic. Greeting card companies are constantly having to find new designs and while some have their own in-house designers or use only reproductions of classic works of art, many more look outside for new designs.

Greeting cards in general encompass a number of different styles: cartoons, watercolours, calligraphic, photographic – spend some time in your local shops analysing what each company specialises in and familiarise yourself with the different styles.

The *Writers' and Artists' Yearbook* lists names and addresses of producers as well as who, and who not, to approach. If you find a make of card which isn't listed, remember that addresses are normally printed on the reverse of each card. Contact the producers to find out if they would be interested in seeing some of your work.

Greeting card design is one area where people in the arts field can make lucrative use of their talents while waiting to be discovered as the next Hockney or Bailey. If you fall into this category you could, in the meantime, have found a way of turning your talents into a profitable business venture.

This will appeal if

- You have artistic/design skills.
- You're a quick worker.
- You can apply your skills to the commercial field.

Advantages

- Low cost start-up.
- Can begin in your spare time.
- Potentially good market (people always want to buy greeting cards).
- You can capitalise on an existing skill.

Disadvantages

- Initially may take some time to place your work.
- Work may be intermittent until you become established.

Future possibilities

- Form a co-operative venture with other designers to extend the range of styles on offer.
- Hire full-time designers.
- Produce your own range of greeting cards.
- Develop the business to include book illustration work, calendars etc.

Address

Writers' & Artists' Yearbook; A & C Black, annual

Way 38 Hairdressing

Hairdressing is one of the traditional areas of self-employment. But with the cost of rents and rates, prospects of setting up a salon may seem less attractive a proposition than before. However, a business which uses your skills can still be established.

Many people don't like going to the hairdressers, are disabled, live too far away, or just don't seem to find the time. There is a potentially huge market consisting of people who would welcome a personal visit. You could travel to their homes or specialise and target business executives at work – perhaps even offering a relaxing scalp massage as an additional service. Contact people direct at their places of work. Hotels may offer opportunities for you as well. The larger ones tend to have their own salons, but smaller ones may appreciate being able to offer an additional service to their guests, perhaps in exchange for a commission from you. Check it out. Patients who have to stay in hospital for longer than a week may offer other opportunities, as well as people in nursing homes.

There are lots of benefits to help sell the service – convenience being the main one. Include them in your sales literature. You could distribute leaflets to houses and place advertisements in your local paper and church magazine, or at Women's Institutes. Word of mouth should eventually bring in lots of custom.

So if you were wondering how to establish yourself as a hairdresser without the money to open a salon, this could be the answer for you.

This will appeal if

- You already have hairdressing skills, or are willing to acquire them.
- You enjoy moving around.
- You're adaptable and can work easily in different places.
- You're reliable and punctual.

Advantages

- Good cash flow set-up.
- Avoids costly salon overheads.
- Repeat business.
- Low cost set-up.

Disadvantages

- Some evening and weekend work.
- Facilities may not be ideal in some people's homes.

- You need transport (not essential, but it will help you to maximise the number of appointments in a day and it means you won't be restricted to one area.)

Future possibilities

- Hire staff to respond to increased workload.
- Train in other skills to expand range of services: massage, nail care, skin-care treatment, waxing.
- Sell other products to clients (see Way 73).
- Establish operations in other areas.
- Develop own range of hair-care products.
- Open a salon(s).

Publications
The Cutting Edge (monthly)
The Hairdressers Journal International (weekly)

Way 39 History of houses

Soon after I moved into my flat an enterprising young man approached me with a photograph of my building at the turn of the century. It had instant appeal and I thought what a huge potential market there must be for what he was doing.

Developing the idea further, you could research local records and find out as much as you can about ownership history, establishing its pedigree, as it were. Describe what daily life was probably like for the first owners, the locality, the type of decor and furniture they would have had, and see if you can find out anything about the individuals themselves.

Think about presentation. If it is just a photograph, have it framed and mounted. If you have written information you could have it typed out onto a scroll or presented in an attractive folder. All this and the time you spend on research must be reflected in the price. Do some careful costings beforehand to make sure you operate at a profit while still offering an attractive price.

Although you could advertise in local papers (they could do an article about you – excellent PR), and by leaflet drops, think about door-to-door selling. I know I couldn't resist seeing what my house looked like in 1897! And perhaps estate agents could offer it as a special service to house buyers, in exchange for a small commission from you.

People are always keen to find out about personal and family histories. Likewise, house histories could fit into this category and form the foundation for a successful business.

This will appeal if

- You're good at research.
- You're good at presenting information.
- You have a sound knowledge of both local and national history.
- You have some selling skills, or are willing to acquire them.

Advantages

- Interesting work.
- Low overheads.
- Low cost start-up.
- Could start in your spare time.
- Good cash flow set-up.
- Once you have researched the information for one area, it can be recycled for other houses.

Disadvantages

- Door-to-door selling, although you don't *have* to start that way.
- Irregular work flow.
- No repeat business.

Future possibilities

- Go up-market. Include those buildings which now house clubs, societies and businesses.
- Publish a book on your research findings.
- Begin to do family trees (see Way 92).

Way 40 House name and number plates

While I was working as a door-to-door market researcher I noticed how many houses were without door numbers or had damaged or illegible name plates. Basement flats also proved difficult: was it Flat 1 or Flat 5; Flat A or E? This lack of clear house-numbering provides an excellent business opportunity for someone.

Select a range of different number and plaque designs. If you're good at handicrafts you could even design some of your own. Cost your materials, and the time it will take to fit them as well.

Finding your customers should be relatively easy. By walking down a street you can see which houses to target. Owner-occupied areas will be your best bet. Post leaflets through doors and call back a day or so later. Be prepared to fit them there and then, or to take an order if it's for a nameplate. Approach businesses and shops, too – their numbering is nearly always inadequate. Think about approaching estate agents who could introduce your service to their clients, whether sellers (to enhance their property) or buyers, and earn themselves a commission too.

This business is a good example of how, when you learn to keep your eyes and ears open, you begin to spot potential business ideas and gaps in the market.

This will appeal if

- You're practical.
- You have some basic selling skills – or are willing to acquire them.
- You're happy working outdoors.
- You have a certain eye for style – you may be expected to advise some customers on the most suitable design.

Advantages

- Quick turn-round of work.
- Potential market is very good.
- Good cash flow set-up.
- Work isn't limited to one area.

Disadvantages

- Some investment in stock needed.
- Requires transport for equipment and stock.

- May require evening and weekend work.
- No repeat business.

Future possibilities

- Expand the range of services: door bell fitting, door knocker replacement, letter box replacement, porch lights, security work (see Way 84) and even door mats.
- Operate as an agent for burglar alarm companies (see Way 73).
- Expand into shop signs.

Way 41 Image consultant

Dressing well depends less on the amount of money you have and more on style and flair. People may have lots of the former, but precious little of the latter. If you have style you could begin to market it and turn it into a successful business.

Periodically, people try to weed out the contents of their wardrobes, but in my experience they end up putting most things back again. This is when your help is needed.

Establish with your client his or her lifestyle, personal style and the sort of budget available. Using this information, survey their wardrobe and advise on which outfits to modify and which to discard. Give advice on how to wear what's left, and what gaps need filling. You could accompany the client on shopping trips or, if some new accessories like scarves or belts are needed, you could do the buying.

Consider how to find those potential customers. It should have lots of up-market appeal and could warrant advertisements in glossy women's, men's, fashion and business magazines. Leave leaflets in hairdressers and clothes shops, perhaps in exchange for a small fee. You could also market yourself by giving talks to groups like Women's Institutes and Chambers of Commerce.

This is a good example of a skill which some may take for granted. Not everyone is capable of finding their style, seeing the potential in clothes and putting successful outfits together. This could be a valuable service for them and an opportunity for you to establish yourself in business.

This will appeal if

- You have good dress sense – for others as well as yourself.
- You enjoy clothes and shopping for them.
- You have excellent interpersonal skills.
- You're good at giving constructive criticism.
- You're patient.

Advantages

- Good working conditions.
- Low overheads.
- Low investment.
- Good cash flow set-up.
- Repeat business.
- New clients through personal recommendation.

Disadvantages

- Irregular work flow.
- May have 'difficult' clients.
- Limited market.

Future possibilities

- Expand the service to include: facials, make-overs, wedding advice, home hairdressing.
- Include a design and dress-making service.
- Establish operations in other locations.
- Acquire premises to run courses.
- Produce and market videos and books.

Publications
The Complete Style Guide, Mary Spillane; Piatkus, 1995
Complete Colour, Style and Image Book, Barbara Jacques; Thorsons, 1996

Way 42 Importing

A friend of mine has worked out a successful way to combine business with pleasure. She regularly travels to her favourite foreign destination, places orders with local craftspeople for goods, imports them and sells them to eager customers back here.

You too could do the same, importing gifts, household goods, clothing, or in fact any items which would find a ready market and prove profitable for you.

There is, however, a lot of research to do beforehand. You need to understand how Customs and Excise affects you, which import licence to apply for from them, freight costs and, using your samples, whether there really is a market for those continental, fluffy whatnots.

Clarify with potential suppliers how quickly they can deliver, and how well they could respond to increased demand and urgent orders. How could they cope with things like colour scheme changes – pink whatnots might not sell, but green ones could take the public by storm!

In terms of your customers you could either sell the goods yourself, perhaps on a market stall (see Way 54) or you could sell to retail outlets. Work out your margins for each one and decide which would be best.

If travel doesn't appeal you could always select products from other countries' trade catalogues. Contact their embassies for details. Whichever way you decide to operate, importing certainly opens up a world of opportunities.

This will appeal if

- You're good at negotiating.
- You can spot market potential.
- You want to combine work with travel.
- You have some selling skills – or are willing to acquire them.
- You're organised.

Advantages

- It combines work with travel.
- Products can attract high premiums.
- Earnings are not limited by your production capacity.

Disadvantages

- Requires investment capital to buy stock.

- Needs storage space for stock.
- Can be a difficult cash flow set-up.

Future possibilities

- Extend your imported range.
- Find suppliers in other countries.
- Open retail outlets.
- Establish retail outlets around the country.

Addresses

British Importers' Association, Suite 8, Castle House, 25 Castlereigh, London W1H 5YR; 0171-258 3999
Board of Customs and Excise, King's Beam House, 39–41 Mark Lane, London EC3R 7HE; 0171-620 1313

Publications
Importing Today (bi-monthly)
Croner's Reference Book for Importers (monthly)
Importers Handbook 91/92, British Importers' Association; Setform Ltd, 1991
Getting Started in Importing, John R Wilson; Kogan Page, 1996

Way 43 Indexing

Before becoming a writer I assumed that indexes in non-fiction books were compiled by the author. Sometimes this is the case, but not always. Authors may not necessarily have the time, inclination or the ability to do the job. Indexing requires specialised skills and you must be fully trained and qualified before being accepted by the Society of Indexers. But afterwards, indexing offers an interesting opportunity for a business with lots of potential to expand.

Once trained you must find your customers. Some may approach you through the Society of Indexers which sends a list of its members each year to major publishers, and also recommends the going rate per hour; but you also need to advertise your specialist service. If there is a subject area of which you already have a good working knowledge, you could approach those publishers who specialise in it. Otherwise, mail non-fiction publishers and book packagers about your service. Advertising in trade journals could be worth considering too – the *Bookseller,* and the Society of Authors' and Writers' Guild's own membership magazines.

Access to a computer will greatly help with this sort of work as well as providing you with an opportunity to do other jobs until the work flow establishes itself and your reputation becomes known. And if you can offer an efficient and reliable indexing service you could find that this may happen sooner than you think.

This will appeal if

- You enjoy reading.
- You enjoy detailed work.
- You're methodical, quick and efficient.
- You have good concentration.
- You have some experience in publishing or books.

Advantages

- Low cost start-up.
- Low overheads.
- Can start in your spare time.
- Repeat business likely once you become established.

Disadvantages

- Some training needed.
- Earnings limited by the amount of work you can do in a day.
- Irregular work flow to start.

Future possibilities

- Extend the range of services to include proof-reading.
- Gradually expand into a full back-up service for writers and publishers: typing, typesetting, proof-reading, research, book design.

Addresses

Society of Indexers, Mermaid House, 1 Mermaid Court, London, SE1 1HR; 0171-403 4947

Book House Training Centre, 45 East Hill, London SW18 2QZ; 0181-874 2718

Publications

Business of Indexing, Pat Booth & Elizabeth Waelis; Society of Indexers, 1989

Indexing, The Art of, Larry S Bonura; John Wiley, 1994

Way 44 Internet businesses

Developments in society inevitably open up opportunities to those entrepreneurs with the skills and imagination to ride the crest of new waves as they appear. The Internet, far from being simply a playground for nerds, is one such development, opening up new business opportunities in a market which is expanding at a phenomenal rate. Areas of growth ripe for the picking may be hard to find elsewhere, so this may be just what you have been looking for.

Internet-related businesses can be split into three categories, the first being those enterprises set up to operate through the Internet for selling products or services. This might include books, magazines, holidays, accounting services, concert and theatre tickets, clothes, legal services and advisory services. In fact, almost anything goes. It seems that if you have something to sell, the Internet is as good a way as any (and better than most) through which to do so. There are even virtual shopping malls. Hire a space just as you would rent a retail space in an ordinary shopping centre but without having to incur the costly overheads like staffing and electricity to worry about – and no shoplifting either. And remember your virtual shop can stay open 24 hours a day throughout the year, plucking customers from around the globe instead of just from around the corner.

The second type of business uses the Internet as a tool to help provide a service to non-Internet customers. This includes any type of research, information and database service. Think about how you might target specific groups of people or businesses who might need the information you can locate but who may not have the time and/or resources to carry out the searches themselves.

The final type of business is at the support level, helping individuals or businesses use the Internet. This can include everything from designing web pages to teaching people how to enjoy trouble-free surfing.

Rarely do new markets arise for small business operators, and never one which has been so truly global. Unlike businesses in the past, location doesn't matter. Wherever you are, think about how you might utilise the opportunities opening up in this virtual marketplace of tomorrow.

This will appeal if

- You enjoy working with computers.
- You are flexible in your thinking and attitude towards business 'environments'.
- Depending on the business, you prefer working with 'virtual' people.

Advantages

- A growth area.
- Depending on the business, has very low overheads compared with traditional ways of operating.
- Depending on the business, location is unimportant.
- Again, depending on the business, you have instant access to a world-wide market.

Disadvantages

- Initial investment in hardware required.
- Must have the necessary skills, or have the funds to buy them in.
- On-going developments also means an on-going investment in skills/software/hardware.
- As the Internet develops, tighter legislation will inevitably be introduced sooner or later which could affect your business.

Future possibilities

- Depends on which sort of business you start, but as the Internet itself grows, so too will your own. As this development takes place, and with your on-going involvement in this medium, remain alert to new opportunities as they arise. One thing is certain; the future possibilities for all businesses in this sector are bound to increase with time.

Publications

30 Minutes to Master the Internet, Neil Barrett; Kogan Page, 1997
Doing Business on the Internet, Simon Collin; Kogan Page, 1997
Guerilla Marketing on the Internet, Jay Conrad Levinson and Charles Rubin; Piatkus Books, 1995
The Internet for Macs for Dummies, Charles Seiter; IDG Books
The Internet for Windows for Dummies, John R Levine and Margaret Levine Young; IDG Books
Internet (monthly)

Way 45 Introducing sidelines

Many shops and businesses offer highly specialised goods and services. Your aim is to introduce new sidelines to them in order to help them increase their profitability – and to make a good profit for your own business too.

For example: introduce towels, soap dishes and other accessories to bathroom fitters and designers; sportsgear and health books to health clubs; combs, slides, earrings and other jewellery to ladies' hairdressers. Spend some time wandering around shops, noting what they stock. Back home, have a few brainstorming sessions about what related items shops could sell and think about which you could provide them with.

Once you have decided on a few items do some more research to find manufacturers' prices, delivery times and so on. Armed with this information you could then begin to operate either as an agent (see Way 73) or as a wholesaler.

Once you develop the habit you will soon find that you can spot opportunities everywhere for introducing new sidelines. This is certainly a business with lots of potential for the real entrepreneur with flair.

This will appeal if

- You have some selling skills – or are willing to acquire them.
- You're a real self-starter.

- You're good at spotting potential.
- You're organised.

Advantages

- Earning potential is high once your customer base is established.
- Potential market enormous.
- As the business progresses, profits increase as you buy in bulk.
- Low cost start-up if you begin as an agent.

Disadvantages

- May need storage space for stock.
- May need investment capital for stock.
- Requires transport for sales calls and possibly for deliveries.

Future possibilities

- With so many different retailers around the country, the possibilities for future expansion into other markets and geographical areas are almost limitless. You may consider setting up fully staffed offices in other localities to break into these areas and devote your own time to managing the continuing expansion of the operation.

Publication
Sell's Products and Services Directory (annual)

Way 46 Inventions

We are surrounded by business opportunities every day of our lives. The secret is in learning how to spot them. This is certainly true about inventions.

How many times have you heard someone say 'This is so tricky/awkward/time consuming'? Each time you hear that, or say it, you are being presented with an opportunity to solve the problem – and make money. All you need is a fertile and creative imagination.

You could concentrate on ideas with mass market appeal, or on products which serve a highly specialised market. If you have spent some time in a particular work setting (including the home) you are in a good position to know what would be most successful.

Simple designs are best, not least because of lower production costs. A wonderful new invention will be no good if people need second mortgages to pay for it and university degrees to use it.

But once you have your idea worked out, contact the local Business Link or Enterprise Unit at your local TEC or LEC for assistance in finding backers or manufacturers (see Useful Addresses). And if yours is a technological innovation you could even apply for the Department of Trade and Industry's SMART award.

This will appeal if

- You're creative.
- You're good at problem solving.
- You're good at translating theories into practice.
- You have good communication skills – you need to be able to communicate your ideas to other people.

Advantages

- Potential earnings could be high.
- Can begin in your spare time.
- Low overheads, assuming someone else is doing the manufacturing.

Disadvantages

- Initially a poor cash flow set-up.
- Some ideas may flop.
- Can be costly and time-consuming registering patents.

Future possibilities

- Develop the initial idea – make it in different colours and sizes, make a portable version or one for children.
- Hire a designer.
- Go into manufacturing.
- Investigate the international market.

Addresses

British Venture Capital Association, Essex House, 12–13 Essex Street, London WC2R 3AA; 0171-240 3849

Institute of Patentees and Inventors, Suite 505a, Triumph House, 189 Regent Street, London W1R 7WF; 0171-434 1818

The Patent Office, Concept House, Cardiff Road, Newport, Gwent NP9 1RH; 0171-438 4700

Institute of Inventors, 19–23 Fosse Way, Ealing, London W13 0BZ; 0181-998 3540/4372/6372. Advice on patents and finding investors.

Publications
How to Make Money from Ideas and Inventions, R Rogers; Kogan Page, 1992

The Patent Office also has a number of useful free booklets.

Way 47 Ironing service

Many things in our daily lives are now automated. Ironing isn't one of them. This is good news because it presents you with a business opportunity to offer a service to all those busy single executives and career-minded couples whose minds are focused elsewhere.

Find your customers by leaflet drops in likely areas, by advertising in local papers and/or newsagents' windows. See if your local launderettes would agree to include one of your leaflets with their service washes, in exchange for a small fee.

Decide whether you will iron 'on site' or operate a collection service. Perhaps you could offer both – elderly people might appreciate the company. If you collect the clothes, can you guarantee a swift service? Could you offer an emergency service? And how will you deal with damages?

Work out your charges per item, building in the delivery costs as well as the time it takes to iron each piece. Be professional and wear a smart, simple uniform to do your collection and deliveries, perhaps even providing bags printed with your business name.

Technology advances at an alarming speed, but until an automatic iron is designed you can be sure that this business could provide you with a steady work flow for a long time to come.

This will appeal if

- You enjoy routine work.
- You have a keen eye for detail.
- You're a quick worker.
- You're organised – Mr X won't want Ms Y's blouses!
- You're reasonably fit.

Advantages

- Low cost start-up.
- Low overheads.
- Good cash flow set-up.
- Repeat business.

Disadvantages

- Repetitious work.
- Earnings are limited by how many shirts you can iron in a day.
- Requires some transport for collection and delivery.

Future possibilities

- Hire staff as workload increases.
- Offer additional services: mending and repairs, dry-cleaning delivery and collection.
- Invest in pressing machines to increase throughput.
- Acquire premises to allow for expansion into a full laundering service.
- Move into the commercial market.

Address

Textile Services Association, 7 Churchill Court, 58 Station Road, North Harrow, Middlesex HA2 7SA; 0181-863 7755. Offers a laundry information service.

Way 48 Letting properties service

With changes in legislation, more rental properties now appear on the market. Also, because of fluctuations in the property market, lots of people have had second thoughts about buying; and, of course, there are many who simply can't afford or don't want to buy. Establishing a letting service to respond to this growing demand is a good example of how a change in trends can lead to a new business opportunity.

The aim of this service is twofold: finding tenants for landlords and properties for tenants. This means that you need two lots of advertising: one to attract tenants and one to attract landlords. Local papers, newsagents' windows, county and up-market magazines are all suitable. You could also contact colleges, universities, embassies, education departments and large corporate clients. Decide which market to specialise in, if any. You may be quite happy dealing with the middle-priced range of properties, or you could decide to handle only up-market properties. Whichever you choose, select the most appropriate advertising vehicle.

Market research should indicate the going rate in your area. It should also reveal what the likely uptake would be and the nature of the competition, thereby helping you to decide on what level to compete: on price, quality of service or type of clientele? Perhaps all three.

Take legal advice on the contracts you use. They should set out clearly the limit of your obligations and liabilities to both landlord and tenant. And with these to hand you should be ready to take advantage of one of the benefits of the recent changes in property market trends.

This will appeal if

- You have good interpersonal skills.
- You're highly organised.
- You're efficient.
- You have a good telephone manner.
- You have some knowledge of current housing legislation – or are willing to find out.

Advantages

- Low cost start-up – you could start with just a telephone and a filing cabinet, although a small office would be better.
- Likelihood of repeat business from satisfied landlords.
- Large potential market.
- Good demand.

Disadvantages

- Irregular workflow.
- May only be suitable for larger towns and cities.

Future possibilities

- Establish branches in other major cities.
- Investigate the European market.
- See also Way 75, Property finding service.
- Offer maintenance service to landlords.
- Acquire your own portfolio of properties to let.
- Graduate into estate agency work.

Publications

Letting Residential Property, Frances M Way; Kogan Page, 1993
Letting Update Journal (quarterly)
Rented Property Weekly

Way 49 Local walks and tours

Leisure is big business. And as the population's disposable income per head increases, and more people retire earlier and live longer, it is getting bigger. Tourism continues to be one of the country's main 'invisible' earners.

You could tap directly into this market with an enterprising business: local town walks and tours.

The trips can be as traditional or off-beat as you want: a pub-crawl around historic inns; a visit to the industrial past; a tour of local artists at work. They can be themed in any way you choose: architecture, events, characters, books, foods, cars – in fact, almost anything goes. Even the most unpromising area probably has something special, something unique to offer, once you start looking.

Be clear in your mind who your customers will be: school children, American tourists, local study groups? This will have a direct bearing not only on the style and content of your package but also on the crucial aspect of advertising. Would advertising in magazines or newspapers abroad be best? Does your local airport/bus/railway station offer any possibilities? Or would advertisements in your local paper be the answer?

What would you want to include in your package: printed itineraries, maps, information sheets, free gimmicks, travel to and from? How would you want to present yourself and your business? Could you tie in with other businesses, eg travel agencies, bookshops, hotels or hotel chains? Above all, ask yourself: 'What will make my tours special?'

This will appeal if

- You like meeting people.
- You're organised and reliable.
- You like routine.
- You're good at remembering facts.
- You're something of an entertainer.

Advantages

- An easy business to maintain.
- Good cash flow element.
- Lends itself to expansion.

Disadvantages

- Repetitious.
- Your work could be adversely affected by weather conditions, seasonal fluctuations, exchange rates, transport problems or international events.

Future possibilities

- Hire and train staff in response to increased workload.
- Develop a more extensive list of packages.
- Develop more comprehensive packages, eg week-long tours including accommodation, national and/or international travel.

Addresses

Contact your regional Tourist Board – address in Yellow Pages.

The Guild of Guide Lecturers, The Guild House, 52d Borough High Street, London SE1 1XN; 0171-403 1115

Way 50 Magazine publishing

Never before has the way into magazine publishing been so open, thanks largely to the advent of computers and the availability of software which now enables more people to put a professional-looking publication together.

While attempting to launch a magazine to compete against the top-selling glossies may be out of your financial spectrum, there is still ample room for magazines which cater to the specific needs of an identified group of individuals, whether pre-school or granny, amateur or professional, for leisure or learning.

Readership is likely to be relatively small if catering to fringe interests, but need not necessarily be less lucrative a venture. Since it is unlikely to find its way onto major newsagents' shelves (only best-selling publications are accepted for a much-coveted place there), sales are more likely to be by subscription which in effect has a positive effect on your cashflow, although it demands more on the marketing side.

But be warned: publishing a magazine demands more than simply being able to wield a desk-top publishing package. Writing, editing, sales, marketing, telesales (finding advertisers), distribution, managing contributors, budgeting, production, planning and scheduling ... Think about where those skills will be found. It is more than likely that at least some will have to be bought in from other sources.

It's also worth reflecting on the fact that a magazine is (hopefully) for life, not just for the first issue. Think about the detailed plans for future issues. How often will the publication appear? Will there be enough accessible and interesting material on a regular basis? How will you find the stories which count?

Think about which niche is waiting, ready for you to serve it with a magazine of its own. And if the readership seems too small to support a lengthy publication, consider setting up a newsletter instead – much less involved, but potentially equally as rewarding.

This will appeal if

- You have a keen interest or background in a particular field or potential readership group.
- You enjoy multi-tasked work.
- You can keep to deadlines.
- You enjoy working under pressure.

Advantages

- Can capitalise on existing skills and interests.
- Revenue from more than one source: cover price and advertising.
- Subscriptions have a positive effect on cash flows.
- Many skill-gaps can be filled by freelancers.
- Provides a ready-made vehicle for promoting other products of your own – books, briefings, consultancy etc.

Disadvantages

- Distribution can be problematic – and costly.
- Accessing your readership to let them know about your publication may be difficult.
- May take longer than expected to build up circulation figures.
- Having to buy in missing skills can be costly.

Future possibilities

- Launch new titles – publishing houses often have a number of magazines under their belt, some acting as a subsidy for other less-lucrative titles.
- Go on the Internet.
- Sponsor conferences, fairs etc.
- Import complementary foreign titles and market them through existing publications.
- Expand into book publishing.

Addresses

Periodical Publishers Association, Queen's House, 28 Kingsway, London WC2B 6JR; 0171-404 4166

Publishers Association, 19 Bedford Square, London WC1B 3HJ; 0171-580 6321

Publications
Directory of Publishing; Publishers Association and Cassell (annual)
How to Publish a Newsletter, Graham Jones; How to Books Ltd, 1992
Magazine Business Weekly Report
Magazine News (bi–monthly)
Publishing (monthly)

Way 51 Mail order

From selling rubber address stamps by mail order, Leonard Carlson now has a business with a turnover of $10 million a year. Of course he branched out over the years and sold other items by post, but his success is still testament to the potential in operating a mail order business.

Products to sell by mail order can include anything from antiques to fine wines; clothes rails to kitchen ware. Almost anything goes. Popular items include books, cosmetics, beauty aids, exercise aids, clothes and gift items. Although some of these are sold by the manufacturers themselves, many are products which have been bought wholesale, produced by other companies or individuals, or imported from abroad.

As with any business, it is important to market research your idea before buying up a warehouseful of items, otherwise you might find your Aunt Mary is the only one interested – and even then only to avoid hurting your feelings. You need to be assured of volume sales or have a good enough mark-up on items to make the venture work.

If you're not sure of how to reach the potential customers you wish to target, look at how the others do it. Where do your competitors advertise their goods? Do they use direct mail? How do they design their literature? What payment terms do they offer? Whatever your well-established competitors are doing, learn from their experience – only do it better.

Once customers start ordering, you are in a position to start building your own mailing list. Winning repeat orders from existing customers is one of the keys to successful mail order businesses. But do note that anyone who holds a database of personal details must register under the Data Protection Act. Also check out the British Code of Advertising Practice which covers those selling by mail order.

This will appeal if

- You live in a remote area and are looking for a business where location is unimportant.
- You are organised and efficient.
- You prefer work which does not involve customer contact.

Advantages

- Avoids costly overheads associated with retail premises.
- Can reach a wider market than having a single shopfront.
- Enables you to start small, even from home.
- Small capital outlay.
- Can be operated from any location. You do not have to be geographically close to your market.

Disadvantages

- May be difficult to anticipate demand in the early days.
- May take some time to build up a customer base for repeat orders.
- Depending on your product, reaching saturation point means other products need to be developed.
- Little or no customer contact (although this may be seen as an advantage for some).

Future possibilities

- Selling on the Internet.
- Developing your range of products.
- Producing a catalogue as the range of products expands.
- Develop an export market to customers abroad.

Addresses

Advertising Standards Authority, Brook House, 2 Torrington Place, London WC1E 7HW; 0171-580 5555

Office of Data Protection Registrar, Wycliffe House, Water Lane, Wilmslow, Cheshire SK9 5AF; 01625 545700

Publications
Running Your Own Mail Order Business, Malcolm Breckman; Kogan Page, 1995
Profit Through the Post, Alison Cork; Piatkus Books, 1994
Catalogue and Mail Order Business (monthly)
Lists and Data Services (bi-annually)

Way 52 Making kits

Many people are tempted to try out new projects but are discouraged by having to find fiddly bits and pieces. Kits solve the problem. If you have an inventive mind you could use this concept as a basis for setting up your own business.

Spend some time looking around at the number of things which are already sold in kit form: furniture, craft items, plant growing, food preparation (scone mixes, pancake mixes) as well as those kits which consist of an assembly of products; for example, computer cleaning and car tuning kits.

There are lots of possibilities, but to help you brainstorm some ideas go to your library and look through craft, gardening, household and DIY books – or indeed any books which you think could yield some ideas. Once you start looking you may find lots of inspiration. Think about topical issues. The 'green' movement could offer some opportunities. Look for those ideas which can easily be developed beyond the basic concept. For example, the ubiquitous egg cosy kit could be developed into different styles: animal, sporting, cartoon and country cottage designs.

When you have identified a few possibilities you need to do some market research and cost production. Would you make them yourself or would you need a manufacturer? The latter has the bonus of giving you more free time in which to concentrate on selling and developing new ideas but is more costly. Conversely you could find an agent to do the selling (see Way 73). And don't forget about packaging considerations too.

Selling things in kit form caters to our continuing desire for convenience, and with a few bright ideas you could soon find yourself running a successful operation based on fulfilling this need.

This will appeal if

- You're inventive, creative and practical.
- You've a logical mind.
- You're organised.
- You enjoy routine work and have a keen eye for detail – if you intend to produce the kits yourself.

Advantages

- Good mark-up on products.
- Could start off in spare time.
- Basic ideas lend themselves to development.
- Kits can be sold by mail order – more lucrative than selling to retail outlets.

Disadvantages

- Some investment in stock needed.
- If selling to retail outlets, cash flow could be difficult.
- Production and storage space needed, if making them yourself.

Future possibilities

- Continue developing product range.
- If producing them yourself, hire outworkers.
- Acquire premises to facilitate increased production.
- Open a kit shop, selling not only your own but other commercially produced kits.
- Open other outlets.

Way 53 Management consultancy

If you have a wealth of experience in business or commerce, you could use it to your advantage and establish your own management consultancy. Small to medium-sized firms will happily pay for access to your valuable experience.

Consider the skills you have. Marketing, PR, customer care, quality and accounting are some of the fields in which you may have expertise. Do your market research to find out what the competition is like, the current market for consultancy, and what the possible uptake could be for your service. Find out what potential customers are looking for. How can you provide it? Could you specialise? For example, an accountant might concentrate on small businesses or a marketing person could target businesses which want to expand into Europe.

Initial meetings with prospective clients are usually free. Based on that meeting, you then normally submit a proposal in which you outline what your consultancy will aim to do, the way in which you will work, the time span and what the fee does and does not include.

You could find clients through personal contacts, advertising in the appropriate business magazines, or you could target specific businesses and write to them personally. Chambers of Commerce, banks, business centres and solicitors could all be useful contacts. However, first jobs are most likely to come from previous employers or through contacts you made while working for them. Without such contacts you could find it very difficult to break into consultancy work successfully.

People tend to take their expertise and hard-earned experience for granted. Make use of yours by establishing yourself as a management consultant and launch yourself into a new business venture.

This will appeal if

- You're experienced and have a good business background on which to build.
- You have good interpersonal skills.
- You enjoy variety.
- You're good at problem solving.
- You enjoy travelling – you will have to go where the work is and projects could involve travelling to outlying branches.
- You're adaptable and flexible.
- You have good writing and presentation skills.

Advantages

- Low overheads.

- Potential earnings very high.
- You can capitalise on the experience you've gained.

Disadvantages

- Intermittent work flow, initially.
- Trying to maintain the difficult balance between 'doing' and 'selling'.

Future possibilities

- Enter into co-operative agreements with others who have business skills and experience complementary to your own.
- Establish a management consultancy with full-time staff.
- Run seminars.
- Investigate the market potential in Europe.

Address

Institute of Management Consultants, 5th Floor, 32–33 Hatton Garden, London EC1N 8DL; 0171-242 2140

Publications
Management Consultancy (monthly)
Start and Run a Profitable Consulting Business, Douglas A Gray; Kogan Page, 1989
101 Ways to Succeed as an Independent Consultant, Timothy R V Foster; Kogan Page, 1991

Way 54 Market stalls

Running a market stall is a good way to start a retail business or test a new product on the buying public. Whatever is your aim you need to find the right market for what you intend to sell, or vice versa. Either way, it is essential you sell what the shoppers are looking for, whether craftwork, imported goods, wholesale goods, food, second-hand items or antiques. And if you have transport you could operate at a different market on each day of the week.

Getting a regular stall can be difficult. Go to the market supervisor (stallholders will tell you where he or she can be found) who will explain how that particular market operates. It could be on a first come, first served basis for casuals. This means that you queue for stall allocation with the attendant risk of being turned down. (Eventually, as a permanent trader, you won't have to do that.) Or you could be placed on a waiting list. The supervisor may want to vet the items you sell. While you're there clarify what the market provides, eg stalls, coverings, lighting.

Once you have your pitch, be prepared with bags to wrap goods in, coin change, business cards, price cards/stickers, notepad and pen, and something to sit on and something to read. Work out your display beforehand too. It should be eyecatching and you may need to buy display stands and/or material with which to cover the base of the stall.

Be helpful and friendly with your customers and if you're selling the right thing in the right place at the right time, you should be sure of a brisk trade.

This will appeal if

- You're an early riser.
- You enjoy working outdoors.
- You enjoy meeting people.
- You're patient – it can sometimes be a long time between sales.

Advantages

- Low overheads.
- Can start in your spare time.
- Good profit margins.
- Can be good fun.

Disadvantages

- Some investment in stock needed.
- May require storage space for stock.
- May require transport.
- Working outdoors in all weathers.

Future possibilities

- Run multiple stalls on more than one market.
- Move into shop premises.

- Open other retail outlets.
- Buy goods direct from manufacturers.
- Run your own market operation.

Address

National Market Traders Federation, Hampton House, Hawshaw Lane, Hoyland, Barnsley, South Yorkshire S74 0HA; 01226 749021

Publications
Market Trader (weekly)
Marketeer (weekly)
Market Trading Annual
Markets Year Book
Running Your Own Market Stall, Dave Hardwick; Kogan Page, 1992

Way 55 Mini cab services

Operating a mini cab service may have little appeal because of the prospect of long hours and unsavoury customers. However, you could establish a specialist service aimed at an identified target group.

Think about the different sectors of your community, both private and commercial. For example, you could form links with local businesses and offer a service which caters to their needs: wear a comfortable 'uniform' suit, provide a copy of the *Financial Times*, have a mobile phone for their use and have travel and local information to hand. Long distance taxi rides might be your speciality.

On the domestic side you could offer a special service to women, operated by women, in which case you could target your advertising through local women's press, health clubs and the Women's Institute.

Market research will uncover target groups. Talk to lots of different people and see if they can provide clues about other possibilities. You should also find out what the competition is like by taking a few rides in their taxis. How could you improve on their service?

The benefit of specialising, besides being able to choose your type of customer and hours of work, is that it makes it easier to find those important customers. Marketing will be easier to plan and more likely to be successful.

So if driving appeals to you, but taxi-ing previously hasn't, take some time to rethink and start brainstorming some ideas to find your own specialised market.

This will appeal if

- You're a good driver and enjoy driving.
- You're presentable.
- You enjoy meeting people.
- You're reliable.
- You've a good memory – for bookings, faces and routes.

Advantages

- Repeat business once you become established.
- Low overheads if you already own a suitable car.
- No investment in stock needed.
- Good cash flow set-up, unless you operate accounts for business clients.

Disadvantages

- Investment in a car if you don't already have one.
- It's a sedentary job.
- Driving all day can be stressful.

Future possibilities

- Acquire other cars to extend the service.
- Establish operations in other localities.
- Operate a limousine or Rolls-Royce service.
- Establish operations to target other specialist groups.
- Diversify into coach hire.

Addresses

Owner Drivers' Society, 21 Buckingham Palace Road, London SW1W 0PN; 0171-834 6541

Publications
Taxinews (9 per year). Owner Drivers' Society
Cab Driver (fortnightly)
Private Hire (monthly)

Way 56 Multi–media design

The technological developments which have seen the introduction of compact discs (CDs) for use on computers have, as a result, also brought with them new business opportunities.

CDs can hold vast amounts of information. This includes not just simple text, but also graphics, animation, illustrations, photographs, sound, film sequences and video footage. There is also ample space for loops, sequences and sub-routines. Businesses have been quick to realise the potential in this for creating quality training materials. This is where you come in as a multi-media designer.

Taking briefs from clients, the multi-media designer plans the overall structure of each training package. This can include creating the script, integrating any existing visuals, identifying the need for other visual images to be included (moving or still), and deciding what other on-screen images should be included to ensure the effectiveness of the training programme. The completed 'design' is then handed over to those with the technical know-how to put the finished product together, although some designers see whole projects through from start to finish if they have the skill and inclination.

Working in multi-media design is like film or video production, within a computer environment. Designers can also be found working on interactive educational materials, promotional materials, interactive CDs for the home and leisure market, and computer games. Another specialism is in designing web pages for companies wishing to go on the World Wide Web. Although some designers operate as independent freelances, approaching companies direct or making use of existing contacts, many others operate through agencies which specialise in this sort of work. They advertise in places like the *Guardian* on Mondays.

Multi-media design is bound to be a growing industry of the future as its full potential becomes harnessed by businesses large and small. This could also be where the potential lies for your own future, and business success.

This will appeal if

- You have a background in training and/or education.
- You are capable of analysing complex problems.
- You are creative with a strong visual sense.

- You have good interpersonal and communication skills.
- You have some understanding of how interactive multi-media works.

Advantages

- Can be very lucrative (£160-£500 per day).
- Is a growing industry.
- Work can be obtained through agencies.
- Multi-media designers are still relatively thin on the ground.

Disadvantages

- You need to have the relevant background and skills.
- Poor client briefing can make the work difficult.
- You need to invest in your own computer – work is normally done off-site, ie in your own place of work.

Future possibilities

Depending on the type of work you do:

- Start your own agency.
- Develop your own products for sale on the open market.
- Run training courses in multi-media design.
- Expand and market your services to potential customers in other countries.
- Hire staff to work under your direction on projects.

Publications
CD–Rom Magazine (quarterly)
Multimedia and CD–Rom Now (monthly)
Multimedia Trade News (monthly)
Multimedia and CD–ROMS for Dummies, Andy Rathbone; IDG Books, 1995

Way 57 Natural toiletry products

With increased 'green' awareness, chemically based products are coming under greater scrutiny from consumers. You could take advantage of this by developing your own range of natural toiletry products.

Although you need no licence to manufacture there are regulations which govern production. (See HMSO publication *Cosmetic Products Safety Regulations* and the 1990 and 1991 amendments; also the Trades Descriptions Act.) But first, what to make? Hair-care products, relaxation and bathtime products, hand creams, skin-care products, body grooming and men's toiletries are all possibilities. Perhaps you can think of some others. Book research should bring recipes to light if your background isn't in cosmetology or chemistry.

Pay attention to packaging. Having it specially designed might be costly, but could pay for itself through increased sales (think of the Body Shop's successful designs). Would additional information also help sell the products – in leaflet form, shelf display information, or packaging information?

Study the competition. Decide if you can compete on price, quality, or presentation. What are your unique selling points (USPs): organic ingredients, continental recipes/formulas, products for executive travellers?

Expand operations slowly, perhaps starting by selling your products on market stalls, or through party plan arrangements, with retail outlets coming later: chemists, health food shops or gift shops, if you're located in or near a tourist area.

However you decide to launch it, this is certainly an area with lots of market potential for you to explore.

This will appeal if

- You're interested in natural products.
- You can follow recipes.
- You have some selling skills – or are willing to acquire them.

Advantages

- An expanding area.
- Lots of potential.
- Good mark-up on products.
- Lends itself to expansion.

Disadvantages

- Competition already exists.
- Investment in stock needed.

Future possibilities

- Acquire manufacturing premises.
- Expand the range of products.
- Investigate export possibilities.
- Open own retail outlets.
- Franchise the operation.
- Produce 'own brands' for supermarket chains.

Addresses

Cosmetic, Toiletry and Perfumery Association, Josaron House, 5/7 John Prince's Street, London W1M 9HD; 0171-491 8891

British Association of Beauty Therapy and Cosmetology, (BAB-TAC), Parabola House, Parabola Road, Cheltenham, Glos GL50 3AH; 01242 570284

Publication
Liz Earle's New Natural Beauty: An illustrated guide to making lotions, balms, tonics and oils; Ebury Press, 1996

Way 58 Nursing home

Recent demographic changes have seen a dramatic and continuing rise in the number of people over the age of 65. Despite the introduction of the community care system which aims to enable people to continue living in their own homes, many still need, or prefer, to live in private residential nursing homes. Although the growth of this sector has been sharpest in previous years, a report by Laing and Buisson, *Care of Elderly People Market Survey 1996*, estimates a continued demand for approximately 38,000 more places by the turn of the century. This obviously signals that there is plenty of room for others to join this specialised sector.

Running a nursing home is very different from managing an ordinary household. Sound management skills are vital to success, or even survival. Costs are high and varied – everything from oxygen cyclinders to special equipment; nursing staff salaries to catering – so the ability to handle complex budgets is of prime importance. One also has to work within the contraints of the many regulations which apply to nursing homes which cover health and safety, the ratio of qualified nursing staff to residents, and also involves registering with your local authority.

Think about the type of person you will be aiming to cater for, whether at the top end of the financial spectrum, with high or low level care requirements, or what about establishing a specialist nursing home for artists, musicians, or some other group of people with common interests or backgrounds? This may simplify your marketing and make for a more harmonious environment for both residents and staff alike.

In this business the hours can be long, crises may occur, and it can leave you feeling drained both physically and mentally. However, this could be how any number of entrepreurs in other businesses would describe their experience of being self-employed. It seems to come with the territory. But the big plus with running a nursing home is that it can be very satisfying work, bringing additional rewards on the personal level difficult to find running other businesses.

This will appeal if

- You have strong management skills.
- You genuinely enjoy elderly people.
- You are fit, if you intend to be involved in the personal care of residents.

Advantages

- Growth sector.
- Rewarding work on the personal level.
- Can live on the premises.

Disadvantages

- High capital outlay, with additional costs to comply with various regulations.
- High overheads.
- Can be very demanding work.

Future possibilities

- Expand into larger premises.
- Establish a group of nursing homes within a locality.

- Investigate the possibility of expanding by franchising the operation.
- Run courses for others interested in running a nursing home.
- Employ a manager to take over the day-to-day running of the home, freeing you to set up another enterprise.

Addresses

Registered Nursing Homes Association, Calthorpe House, Hagley Road, Edgbaston, Birmingham B16 8QY; 0121-454 2511

Royal College of Nursing, 20 Cavendish Square, London W1M 0AB; 0171-409 3333

Publications
Care Home Proprietor (quarterly)
Caring Times (monthly)
Caring Today (bi–monthly)
Nursing Times (weekly)
Guide to Setting Up and Managing a Residential Home, Jenyth Worsley; Age Concern, 1992

Way 59 Office equipment cleaning

Like everything else, office equipment gets dirty. Static soon builds up, making computer screens, keyboards and panels grimy. Office cleaners tend to overlook machines, concentrating on floors and surfaces instead. Equipment users seldom have the time or inclination to do the job either, their time being more valuably employed elsewhere.

Your service could specialise in filling this gap in the cleaning market, with contracts offering a regular cleaning service of computers, fax machines, telephones and switchboards – just some of the machines commonly found in offices. Contact manufacturers to check recommended cleaning routines, procedures and materials.

Find customers through direct mail, perhaps followed up with telephone calls. But before you do this, market research your service. Only if all looks well are you then ready to start marketing.

Besides listing cleaning charges per item, remember to sell the benefits of the service: a healthier working environment (eg reducing the possible spread of infection by telephones), improving the overall working environment and impressing customers. Businesses also have the assurance that competent staff will be doing the cleaning, making sure that computers aren't interfered with and buttons which really ought not to be pressed are left alone. Reinforce this professional image by wearing a simple, clean-looking uniform printed with your business name. Who knows? – tomorrow it could become the byword for clean office equipment.

This will appeal if

- You enjoy cleaning and take a pride in it.
- You have a keen eye for detail.
- You're careful and are sensible about machines.
- You enjoy routine work.

Advantages

- Regularity of work.
- Low start-up costs.
- Low overheads.
- Good cash flow set-up.
- Light duty work.

Disadvantages

- May have to work outside normal office hours.
- Access to equipment may be difficult.
- Earnings limited by the number of hours you can work.

Future possibilities

- Hire more staff in response to increased work-flow.
- Expand into other localities.
- Extend the range of services, selling eg desk supplies, general cleaning.
- Develop and market your own range of office equipment cleaning materials and products.

Publication
Your Guide to Simple Computer Maintenance and Repair, John Farrier and Robert Jukes; Cappell Bann Publishing, 1993

Way 60 Office lunches

Many workers find lunchtimes difficult. They may work in out-of-the-way locations, far away from sandwich bars or cafés. Or they may find it tiresome pushing through high street crowds and queuing. Or they may be too busy to go out to buy their favourite 'egg mayonnaise with salad, on brown.' All are potential customers for your sandwich lunch service.

To operate this business you will need a food-handling licence from the Environmental Health Officer. Apply at your local town hall.

Do your market research to find the likely uptake and best area for your rounds. Some larger businesses and factories have their own canteen facilities and you need to know which ones.

You could phone businesses to see if they would be interested, or you could simply turn up with sandwich supplies and hope. But when they see your delicious looking food, tastefully presented, they are bound to be tempted. You could also consider delivering a selection of free sandwiches to launch your service.

As you get to know people's likes and dislikes it will become easier to judge how many cheese and chutney and ham salad to prepare each day. Eventually you could try introducing new, more exotic lines, offering an organic selection, and carrying soft drinks and confectionery. However you operate, don't skimp on fillings. Well-filled sandwiches are always popular; thin, sad ones aren't.

Besides making sure that the food is well presented (include free serviettes, printed with your business name) people will associate your personal presentation with the quality of the food. Wear a simple, spotlessly clean 'uniform' printed with your business name and always make sure that you're tidy and spotlessly clean too.

This will appeal if

- You enjoy early morning work.
- You enjoy routine.
- You're a quick worker.

Advantages

- Low overheads.
- Good cash flow set-up.
- Regular work once customer base is established.

Disadvantages

- Some transport needed.
- Requires preparation space.
- Earnings limited to the five-day week and the morning/lunchtime period.

Future possibilities

- Develop other rounds, using hired help.
- Extend the range of services (see Way 16)
- Establish operations in other towns.
- Open a high street sandwich shop.
- Franchise the operations.

For useful addresses and publications see Way 16, Catering service

Way 61 Organic food supplier

Organic foods form a significant growth area, enough to prompt some supermarkets to begin stocking a limited range. But although consumers may want to buy, finding a retailer can be difficult and even then prices are often prohibitive – organic foods tend to attract high premiums.

You could carve a niche for yourself by supplying households direct with fresh organic produce – without those high premiums.

Market research the idea in your area. From the information you gather you will be able to decide which areas to target and what to charge. Decide how to operate. Will you take telephone orders or will you deliver a vegetable pot-luck box, a fruit one or a mix of both, perhaps in a choice of £5/£10/£15 boxes? Running a market stall is another possibility.

For a delivery service, advertise in local papers or do leaflet drops. Health food shops which don't stock organic foods may be willing to distribute leaflets for a small fee. Remember to stress the benefits of your service in all advertising – healthier eating, fresher food, convenience of deliveries, the savings to be made.

In keeping with the 'green' spirit, re-use delivery boxes (perhaps printed with your business name). And what about a horse and cart for transport? It would be excellent marketing as well as being environmentally sound – check out the costs first. But at the end of the day it will be the produce, the benefits and quality of service which will help ensure a successful business venture.

This will appeal if

- You're organised.
- You enjoy routine work.
- You enjoy driving (or are good with horses!).
- You're reasonably fit.
- You'd like to contribute to the 'green' movement.

Advantages

- Good cash flow set-up.
- Regular work once your customer base is established.
- Low overheads.
- Increasing public awareness of benefits of organic foods.

Disadvantages

- Requires transport.
- Requires space to store food, take deliveries and make up orders.
- Earnings limited by the number of deliveries you can make in a day.
- Costly wastage of spoiled, unsold stock.

Future possibilities

- Establish bigger rounds.
- Expand range of supplies to include products like 'green' household cleaners and organic bread.
- Deal direct with growers if not doing so already.
- Open an organic vegetable shop.

- Franchise the operation.
- Run your own organic farm.

Address

Soil Association, 86 Colston Street, Bristol BS1 5BB; 01179 290661

Way 62 Organising conferences

Small to medium-sized businesses, while not in the same league as corporate businesses, still need to hold conferences of one sort or another.

Your business offers to organise the event. You recommend the most suitable venue and organise transport, maps and accommodation, if necessary. You handle the conference literature, including any invitations. You also find out what specific facilities are needed at the venue and organise them: refreshments, facilities for disabled people, writing equipment, audio-visual aids, video-recording facilities, display boards, to name a few. You have to be highly organised to run this business successfully – and so do your suppliers. Check them out thoroughly beforehand. The professionalism of their service will reflect on your own.

A nice touch, which will also help to promote your business, is to have free folders, pens, pencils and notepaper printed with your business name, address and telephone number. But in terms of advertising to find customers, business magazines, your local paper if it has a business section, and mailshots are all worth investigating. Contact your local Chamber of Commerce as well. You could advertise in its magazine and possibly mail its members. Check it out.

Once up and running, this is certainly a business which will keep you busy. If you thrive on this sort of work and you're well organised, it could be the one for you.

This will appeal if

- You're organised and efficient.
- You have good project management skills.
- You're good at meeting deadlines.
- You're able to talk at board level.
- You have a professional attitude.

Advantages

- Low cost start-up.
- It pays well.
- Can run more than one conference at a time.

Disadvantages

- Can be highly pressurised.
- Work flow can be irregular.
- Can be affected by economic down-turns.

Future possibilities

- Move up-market, organising conferences for larger companies.
- Acquire a conference centre with full facilities, from meeting rooms to a conference hall.
- Acquire supply businesses, eg catering, printing, design, and audio-visual operations.

Address

ACE United Kingdom, Riverside House, High Street, Huntingdon, Cambs PE18 6SG; 01480 457595. For information about all aspects of organising conferences, exhibitions and events.

Publications
Conference and Exhibition Fact Finder (monthly)
How to Organise Effective Conferences and Meetings, David Seekings, 6th edition; Kogan Page, 1996
Complete Conference Organiser's Handbook, Robin O'Connor; Piatkus, 1994

Way 63 Party DJ

Parties and celebrations often include music for entertainment, plus a suitable DJ. If you enjoy music and this appeals to you as a business, read on.

Firstly, consider the many different types of function for which you might be booked: weddings, 18th and 21st birthday celebrations, office parties. You may have to cater for a wide range of music tastes – unless you decide to specialise and target one particular group. If your market research supports this idea then do so. Your research should also indicate the local going rate and unearth venues which might be interested in hiring you.

You will probably find customers through advertisements in local papers. But also contact pubs, clubs, societies, larger businesses, schools, charities, colleges, churches and any others who you think might be interested, such as catering firms. Once you become known, the majority of your work will be repeat business and by recommendation.

Giving a professional service involves more than simply turning up on the night. Clarify with the customer what sort of event it is, the type of people attending, the itinerary, preferred music, and so on. You also need to check out the premises if you're unfamiliar with them. In this way you ensure that your performance is professional and contributes not only to the success of the evening but also to the ultimate success of your own business.

This will appeal if

- You enjoy music and entertaining people.
- You enjoy evening work.
- You have a good knowledge of a wide variety of music.
- You're an extrovert.
- You're fit.
- You can drive.
- You're flexible.

Advantages

- Possibility of regular work if you can find a 'residency'.
- Low overheads.
- Good cash flow set-up.
- Can start in your spare time.

Disadvantages

- Some seasonality, peaking around Christmas.
- Requires investment in equipment.
- Late night working. It can affect your own social life.

Future possibilities

- Invest in additional equipment and hire staff to cover other areas.
- Extend the services you offer to include catering, karaoke hire, marquee hire etc.
- Acquire your own premises for hire.
- Open a night club.

Addresses

The Performing Rights Society, 29–33 Berners Street, London W1P 4AA; 0171-580 5544. For details of royalty payments for playing records.

Phonographic Performance Ltd, 14–22 Ganton Street, London W1V 1LB; 0171-437 0311. For details of licences for operating mobile discos.

Publications
Freelance DJ-ing, John Clancy; How To Books, 1996
Disco Mirror and Licensed Design (monthly)
Disco Club and Leisure International (monthly)

Way 64 Party planning

If you have ever held a party for more than just a handful of guests you will realise just how much hard work is involved. It is understandable that people planning more impressive, formal or larger parties may decide to hire someone to do it for them.

Think about the sorts of things you may be asked to handle: food, drink, entertainers, entertainment (games, themes etc), venues, transport, invitations, overnight accommodation, waiters/waitresses, marquees, tables, chairs, fancy dress hire. Need I go on? But before you decide you couldn't possibly do all that, the party organiser's role is not to do the buffet/entertainment/waiting themselves. Instead, you co-ordinate the activities of the professional firms with which you will be dealing. Finding reliable, high quality suppliers will be an important part of your work. Interpersonal and project management skills of a high order, and the ability to stay calm at all times, are prerequisites for this sort of business.

Advertise your services through up-market glossies like *Tatler* and county magazines. You could also contact likely businesses, societies, charities, clubs, and any other organisations and notable individuals who might be interested in your service.

Think about launching the business in time to take advantage of the Christmas season. And when people see the high quality service you offer you could begin to see the start of a flourishing business success.

This will appeal if

- You have excellent management skills.
- You're calm.
- You're highly organised and efficient.
- You have a professional attitude.

Advantages

- Low overheads.
- Low start-up costs.
- Varied work.

Disadvantages

- Irregular work-flow to start.
- Some unsocial hours.
- Can be highly stressful.

Future possibilities

- Hire managers to run additional bookings.
- Acquire or establish supply businesses: catering, fancy dress, wines and spirits etc.
- Expand into conference work (see Way 62).

Way 65 Personalised gifts

Personalised gifts have always been popular. One prestigious shop in London specialises in monogrammed items. Another has opened offering an embroidery service for personalising a whole range of products from handkerchiefs to bath towels. The demand for this service is there.

You could use your own skills to personalise gifts. Are you good at calligraphy, glass or metal engraving, needlework or pokerwork? There is an almost unlimited number of gift items with which you could work – either handmade or manufactured. You could market research novel ideas too. I remember seeing an outlet in Australia where the artist applied personalised cartoons in waterproof inks to T-shirts. His business was positively thriving.

There are also mechanical ways to personalise gifts. Small desktop embossing machines which can print on to a wide range of objects could be the answer if your artistic talents are somewhat lacking. Pens, pencils, key rings, cards and credit card wallets are just some of the popular items you could market.

There are many different areas in which to specialise – from expensive gifts with handworked lettering right through to mass-produced, inexpensive ones. The marketing for each will obviously be different. Volume sales could be aimed at hotels, charities, conference centres and businesses. With individual gifts you need to find retailers to take your goods and operate the personalisation service with you; or you could offer a mail order service. Again, think who your customer is and advertise in the appropriate glossy magazine or newspaper.

From a basic concept, personalising gifts offers a vast range of opportunities. Work out costs and keep an eye on them, but remember that personalising increases the perceived value of any gift – a benefit much to your business's advantage.

This will appeal if

- You enjoy repetitive work.
- You have some artistic abilities.
- You're a quick worker.
- You have a keen eye for detail.
- You have some selling skills, or are willing to acquire them – or you could use an agent (see Way 73).

Advantages

- Could begin in your spare time.
- Good cash flow if by mail order.
- Repeat business likely.
- Personalising appears to remain popular.

Disadvantages

- Depending on method of personalising, some investment in equipment could be needed.
- Requires some investment in stock.

Future possibilities

- Hire additional staff to meet increased demand.
- Expand product range.
- Acquire shop premises, specialising in personalised gifts.
- Establish branches in other locations.

Publication

Kompass UK; (annual). A directory of manufacturers' products and services.

Way 66 Personal trainer

A growing trend already well-established in the States is for people who want to get fit to hire their own personal trainer. The appeal is understandable, bringing with it both savings and covenience. Joining the more up-market health clubs can be costly, and time-consuming for people with busy schedules. Having a personal trainer visit them at their home makes getting or keeping fit that much easier.

Having a keen interest in exercise is important, but being a personal trainer will also involve you in performing fitness tests on new clients, working out a suitable exercise programme for them, being aware of health and safety considerations, and basic nutrition as well, so you need to know what you're doing. You will need to attend a short course to gain the appropriate training and qualifications before setting up in business. See below for details.

Potential clients for this service include busy executives, amateur and professional sportspeople, new mums wanting to regain their waistline and people wanting to get fitter for health reasons. You may find yourself conducting sessions in people's offices as well as in their homes. Appointment times and the fees you charge need to take into account travel time between clients.

Once you start to become established, new clients should come by word of mouth, but initially advertisements in local papers, mailings to business executives or leaflet drops to addresses in your local area will all help. So too will pinning your business card to noticeboards in gyms, health clubs, doctors' surgeries, health food shops and other places where it is likely to catch the attention of your target client group.

This can be a very rewarding business to run, bringing with it both financial and personal rewards in helping others become fitter and healthier. If you enjoy exercise and keeping fit yourself, this could be the perfect way into self-employment.

This will appeal if

- You enjoy exercise and keeping fit.
- You like working with people on a one-to-one basis.
- You are good at motivating people and giving encouragement.
- You have a cheerful personality.
- You like routine.

Advantages

- No costly overheads of business premises. This business can be run from your home.
- Low cost start-up.
- Once established, clients can come by word of mouth.
- Rewarding work.
- Can be run on a part-time basis.

Disadvantages

- May take time to build up a client base.
- Involves a lot of travelling.
- Requires qualifications to enter the profession.
- Can be tiring work.

Future possibilities

- Hire other personal trainers to work for you.
- Expand into other localities, perhaps operating as a franchise.
- Design your own range of keep fit outfits.
- Produce keep fit videos.
- Buy a gym or health club.

Addresses

National Coaching Foundation, 114 Cardigan Road, Headingley, Leeds LS6 3BJ; 0113 274 4802

Sports Council, 16 Upper Woburn Place, London WC1H 0QP; 0171-273 1500

Publications
Fitness (annual)
Ultra-fit (bi-monthly)
Work-Out (monthly)
How to be a Personal Trainer: A step by step guide to setting up your business, getting clients and designing specialised fitness programmes, Martica Heaner; Artichoke & Frederick, 1991

Way 67 Pet food supplier

Anyone with a cat or dog will tell you how heavily cans of pet food weigh down the weekly shopping bag. As a cat owner myself I would happily subscribe to a service which could also deliver even heavier cat litter. I imagine dog biscuits are also a weighty problem. Your service could offer to deliver pet foods and supplies direct to people's doors.

Finding customers should present few difficulties but do some research beforehand into the likely uptake. You could ask local vets to hand out advertising leaflets to clients, in exchange for a small fee. You could also advertise in local papers, church and county magazines.

You will be buying in bulk and therefore need storage and transport. However, your overheads should still be lower than supermarkets'. Research into costs and aim to sell at competitive rates. However, having said that, people will be buying convenience and may be willing to pay slightly more.

Another unique selling point (USP) could be to offer fresh meat and bones. I know of no supermarket which sells fresh petfoods so this could be the competitive edge you've been looking for. Negotiate deals with suitable butchers who may be willing to package the food for you as well.

All in all this service offers lots of opportunities. Could you turn it into a thriving and successful business?

This will appeal if

- You're fit.
- You enjoy driving.
- You enjoy routine work.
- You're organised.

Advantages

- Good cash flow set-up.
- Relatively low overheads.
- Regular work once customer base is established.

Disadvantages

- Requires transport and storage space.
- Not much variety.
- Difficult (but not impossible) to take time off because of commitment to delivery schedules.

Future possibilities

- Run a fleet of vans to cover different areas.
- Extend the range of supplies to include things like collars, flea sprays, leads, food bowls etc.
- Franchise the operation.

Addresses

Pet Care Trust, Bedford Business Centre, 170 Mile Road, Bedford MK42 9TW; 01234 273933

Publications
Pet Product Marketing (monthly)
Pet Business World (monthly)

Way 68 Pet sitting and walking

Pet owners have a problem. What do they do with Fido when they go on holiday, make short business trips or are called away unexpectedly? Friends, relatives and neighbours may not always be available and good catteries or kennels can be difficult to find, upsetting for animals, and inconvenient for owners who have to spend valuable time driving to out-of-the-way locations.

There appears to be a gap in the market for a pet-sitting service – looking after animals in their own home.

Stress the many benefits in your advertisements and sales literature: less disruption for pets; peace of mind for owners; cheaper than boarding; removes obligation from friends/families/neighbours; last-minute placements less of a problem; convenience.

The one thing potential customers may be wary about is leaving keys with a stranger. To reassure them, have copies of references available: one from a person of some note and the other from a customer. Check that referees would be happy for people to phone them.

You may like to have a formal contract drawn up by your solicitor to cover and limit your liabilities. Clients can sign it when you meet to discuss feeding and exercise routines, who will be responsible for buying food and supplies, and who their vet is.

People care a lot about their pets. The thought of leaving them in kennels or catteries can be distressing and may not always meet the demands of unexpected situations. If you like animals, pet sitting has lots of benefits to help you turn it into what could be a flourishing business.

This will appeal if

- You're good with, and like, animals.
- You're organised.
- You're reliable.
- You're reasonably fit.
- You're conscientious.

Advantages

- Repeat business likely once customers have used your service.
- Very low overheads.
- Very low cost start-up.
- Good cash flow set-up.

Disadvantages

- Some seasonality to work (busier in summer holidays).
- May need some form of transport.
- Earnings are limited by the number of animals you can look after in a day.
- Some evening and weekend work.

Future possibilities

- Hire staff to cover wider areas and additional workload.
- Offer a wider range of services: grooming, exercising, training, delivering pet food supplies (see Way 67).

Publication
Petlife Magazine (bi-monthly)

Way 69 Picture library

The media, including television and video production companies, newspapers, publishers, advertising agencies, book packagers and magazine publishers all use photographs. Not all of those you see in print have been specially commissioned. For speed and range of choice some will have come from picture libraries.

If your photographic skills are up to scratch, you could put them to use by running your own picture library. For an immediate start you will need to have a large collection of pictures which are of top grade, printing quality.

There are well-established general picture libraries and others which specialise in a particular area (use them to research the going rates). If you have an abiding interest in, and knowledge of, a particular subject area this could be your way forward.

Take legal advice in drawing up your terms of business to include:

- *Search fees* — How much you charge for locating photographs.
- *Holding fees* — What to charge if they keep the photos beyond the agreed period, eg one month.

• *Damage/loss*	How much to charge.
• *Reproduction rights*	UK, world rights, size, front cover usage etc.
• *Payment dates*	On publication or in six months.
• *Liabilities*	Who is responsible, and when.

People have to know you're there, so publicity is important. Do mail shots to publishers and photo users whom you could supply, and freelance picture researchers who could use you.

Once established as providing a prompt, high quality service, your workload should become more regular. Keep clients up to date about new stock as you expand, and with time you should see your business expand its profits too.

This will appeal if

- You're a good photographer.
- You have a subject specialism – or could develop one (or two).
- You're highly organised.
- You're reliable.
- You have a large stock of high quality photographs.

Advantages

- Each photograph has, theoretically, unlimited earning potential.
- Low overheads.
- Opportunities to create market niches.

Disadvantages

- Initial investment in camera and film stock needed.
- A difficult cash flow to begin with because of the long delay in payments – anything up to a year.
- Initially, irregular work flow.

Future possibilities

- Continued expansion of photographic stock.
- Acquire photographs from other sources.
- Hire staff to run the administrative side.
- Historical events and rare photographs (say of famous people

in unusual poses) command high premiums. You could develop a lucrative second specialism in this area alone.

Address

British Association of Picture Libraries and Agencies (BAPLA), 18 Vine Hill, London EC1R 5DX; 0171-713 1780

Publication
BAPLA Directory; BAPLA (annual)
A directory of members, subject index and practical guide for libraries.

Way 70 Premium rate telephone lines

This is a good example of how technological advances in one field open the door to new business opportunities in others.

Premium rate telephone lines, like BT's Callstream 0898 numbers, are used to provide callers with information or advice, or to promote businesses. Although expensive compared with the cost of standard telephone tariffs, people are willing to pay extra for information that they need. Each month you receive a proportion of the cost which has been charged to each caller.

Potential areas are wide-ranging and diverse, offering many opportunities. Financial services already form one large sector; leisure and recreation another. You may be able to come up with some new idea to access unexplored markets within these fields.

There are a number of restrictions in setting up an operation, concerning the minimum number of lines to be rented and the income each must generate. Also, the Code of Practice laid down by the Independent Committee for the Supervision of Standards of Telephone Information Services (ICSTIS) is designed to protect the public from rogue operators.

Like any other business, market research and drawing up cash flow projections are important. Marketing the service will be something else for you to consider. However, once it's up and running, you can sit back, wait for the payments to come in, and perhaps start to plan your next money-making project.

This will appeal if

- You have bona fide credentials for offering advice or information.
- You would like a business which runs itself.
- You prefer a business which does not involve direct selling.

Advantages

- Low maintenance business.
- It offers lots of untapped potential.
- Depending on the subject matter, you could have a potentially huge market.

Disadvantages

- High start-up costs.
- May not reach the threshold income for each line.
- Little involvement once established.

Future possibilities

- Increase the appeal of your recording by hiring 'famous' people to do the readings.
- Develop other lines once you have proved the success of your first one.
- Set up an agency to help others break into the market, organising the production of the recorded messages and devising marketing strategies for them.

Addresses

Mercury Communications Ltd; Freecall 0500 700101

BT Callstream Services, NSS 3.5, 8th Floor, Tenter House, 45 Moorfields, London EC2Y 9TH; 0800 282282

Contact them for their free brochure packs which explain in detail about setting up premium rate numbers.

Way 71 Print selling

Although I love books and take great care with them, I have to acknowlege that they can reach a stage beyond use and repair.

Print selling uses this opportunity to break books apart and remove illustrations for mounting or framing.

To succeed you need access to a constant supply of books. Think about advertising for them, attending book auctions, rummaging through household effects at auction; you could even find out what second-hand bookshops and places like Oxfam do with the books they can't sell.

Market stalls might be ideal for this venture (see Way 54), or you could sell to retail outlets. Interior designers for both commercial and private properties might also provide another market. And what about approaching garden centres with a supply of floral prints; pet shops with illustrations of cats and dogs?

As you become more experienced, you could choose to specialise in, say, children's book illustrations, natural or local history prints. Watch what sells best and tailor your stock accordingly.

If this business appeals, you must do some homework first. Some books, even though they may seem worthless to you, might be valuable and breaking them apart would be the worst thing to do.

This will appeal if

- You have a good eye: for picking out saleable prints and for telling a good reproduction from a bad one.
- You're a neat worker – to mount and/or frame the prints. Presentation is important.

Advantages

- Low investment in stock – you'll be using what others can't sell.
- Excellent mark-up and potential profit.
- Could start part time.

Disadvantages

- It could take a while to build up initial stock.
- You could break a valuable book.
- Little repeat business if running a market stall.

Future possibilities

- Acquire shop premises.

- Reprint illustrations and sell copies in bulk. Check with the Copyright Licensing Agency (CLA) first about copyright.
- Develop your own range of greeting cards, calendars and other stationery items using the illustrations. (Again check with the CLA).
- Trade up-market; deal in original artwork and rare prints.

Addresses

Ephemera Society, 84 Marylebone High Street, London W1; 0171-935 7305

Copyright Licensing Agency, 90 Tottenham Court Road, London W1P 0HE; 0171-436 5931

Publication
Antiques Trade Gazette (weekly paper with details of auctions)

Way 72 Private investigation agency

Television and film has given us a rather romantic image of private investigators. The reality is somewhat different, but if you have legal experience, have worked in security, have done other investigative work or even have a good business background, you could have the credentials for this sort of work.

Some of what you do will be routine, such as serving writs on people. More interesting jobs could involve tracing missing persons, investigating the backgrounds of applicants for sensitive posts, and industrial espionage.

Although you can study for a qualification through the Institute of Professional Investigators Ltd, anyone can set up in this business. All you need is a small office, an answerphone, a camera and a typewriter for writing regular reports to your clients.

As with any other business, you need to do your market research. Test your detective skills by finding out about competitors, the going rate, and the potential market where you live. You also need to think about your professional image and how to market yourself. Local solicitors, businesses and debt collection agencies could be some of your clients. Mail them direct and advertise in Yellow Pages. If you already have personal contacts, so much the better.

Private investigation work is rarely as thrilling as the media would have us believe. But it can be exciting setting up your own business, and this could be the one for you.

This will appeal if

- You have good research/investigative skills.
- You have good interpersonal skills.
- You're sharp.
- You enjoy variety.
- You have some knowledge of the legal system.

Advantages

- Low cost start-up.
- No specialist skills or qualifications needed.
- Can be interesting work.
- Can utilise your own relevant experience.

Disadvantages

- Irregular work flow.
- May be difficult to become established.
- Can involve unsocial hours and, yes, you may meet difficult people.

Future possibilities

- Begin to specialise and build a reputation in a specific field, eg industrial espionage.
- Employ additional staff to respond to increased workload.
- Set up a correspondence course.
- Establish a training school.
- Write about your work.

Addresses

Institute of Professional Investigators Ltd, 31a Wellington Street, St Johns, Blackburn, Lancs BB1 8AF; 01254 680072

Association of British Investigators, ABI House, 10 Bonner Hill Road, Kingston upon Thames, Surrey KT1 3EP; 0181-546 3368

Way 73 Product agent

People running small businesses seldom have the in-house expertise to sell their goods, nor do they have the money to hire full-time sales people. As an agent you solve the problem by offering to sell their products in exchange for a commission on the orders you win.

Before you dismiss a selling job out of hand, it is worth pointing out that it is mainly about two things: enjoying meeting people, and believing in the product. So read on.

As an agent your involvement is limited. You make the sale, take the order, pass it on, collect your commission, then eventually return to take another order. Invoicing and delivery are left to the supplier. However, good agents look after their customers by chasing things along and keeping in close contact.

There is no commitment to sell just one business's products. Build a portfolio of complementary products to maximise your chances of making at least one sale on each call. For example, sell ornaments *and* gift-wrap. Choose products from a field you're familiar with, or those which you could enthuse about. And when you have found your suppliers, agree territories, commission rates, payment schedules, and so on.

Look after your customers, know the products well, and be professional in all your dealings. Once you start the ball rolling, you could be pleasantly surprised at how enjoyable and lucrative an agency can be.

This will appeal if

- You enjoy meeting people.
- You're organised.
- You're enthusiastic.
- You're punctual.

Advantages

- Low cost start-up.
- Flexible hours.
- You have control over what you sell.

Disadvantages

- Waiting up to six months for your commission.
- You may lose customers if your suppliers provide a poor service.
- Ideally, you need a car.

Future possibilities

- Hire staff to cover larger areas.
- Investigate opportunities in the European market.
- Branch into more diverse product areas.

Addresses

Manufacturers' Agents' Association (MAA), 1 Somers Road, Reigate, Surrey RH2 9DU; 01737 241025

British Agents Register, 24 Mount Parade, Harrogate, Yorks HG1 1BP; 01423 560608. Operates a matching service.

Publications
The Manufacturers' Agent (bi-monthly)
BAR Review (monthly magazine from British Agents Register – see above)
How to Become a Freelance Sales Agent, Terry James; How to Books, 1996

Way 74 Professional's manager or agent

There are lots of gifted people around who are excellent at their craft but who fail at self-management and self-promotion. This is what you, as an agent or manager, hope to do for them in exchange for a percentage of their earnings.

Your role is to organise them, find markets for their work, build and maintain their profile, negotiate on their behalf, and generally look after their interests. You could decide that you would rather just sell their work or make bookings for them, but the more you can offer the better.

Experience in the relevant field is essential. If you don't have any, delay your start-up while you get some and make your plans more long term instead. Think of the additional time you spend working in the right environment as an investment in your future business. However, having said that, I am sure there are people who have set out with no such prior knowledge and still succeeded.

You may be able to find clients through personal contacts, advertising in appropriate newspapers or magazines or by finding them at art college shows, craft fairs, live music venues etc. And when you have found that talented someone, ask your solicitor to draw up the appropriate contract.

The other side of the business depends on your PR abilities. Can you promote your artist? If you are good and become established as someone who consistently handles quality work/artists your reputation will soon become known and the hard push will be less necessary.

This can be an incredibly demanding field in which to work, but with the right degree of knowledge, PR and management skills it could be the business for you.

This will appeal if

- You have relevant experience of your chosen field.
- You have good interpersonal and negotiating skills.
- You're astute.
- You have a good eye for spotting talent and potential.
- You're organised.
- You're persistent.

Advantages

- Low cost start-up.
- Can handle a number of clients at once.
- Potentially excellent earnings – one of your clients could be the next Hockney, Madonna or Jackie Collins!
- Low overheads.

Disadvantages

- Intermittent work flow to start.
- Possibly a difficult cash flow – you have to wait for the artist to be paid before you receive your share.

Future possibilities

- Acquire office premises.
- Promote clients abroad.
- Expand the range of services to clients, ie full management and promotion.
- Employ additional staff as work flow increases.
- Establish operations in other parts of the country.

Addresses

Association of Authors' Agents, Secretary, 37 Goldhawk Road, London W12 8QQ; 0181-749 0315

Entertainment Agents' Association, Room 54, Keyes House, Dolphin Square, London SW1V 3NA; 0171-834 0515

Personal Managers' Association, 1 Summer Road, East Molesey, Surrey KT8 9LX; 0181-398 9796

Way 75 Property finding service

Estate agents do a valuable job in introducing potential buyers to sellers. However, they are limited by the number of properties they may have on their books at any one time and buyers often have to contact a number of agents. This can be very time consuming. A property finding service cuts through the problem.

You operate by finding out from clients exactly what they are looking for: type of property, location, number of bedrooms, price range, access to gardens and so on. Compile a shortlist of suitable properties for them to view. As we all know, the 'charming flat with lots of character' can turn out to be an absolute hell-hole! So there will be lots of footwork and careful assessment before recommending to your clients that they take time out of their busy schedules to view.

You will not only be scouring estate agents' lists, but also private sales advertised in local papers, auction lists, *Dalton's Weekly* and Sunday papers. Think about where else you might see property advertised.

Consider who your clients will be: rather than 'ordinary' property buyers they will be people relocated by employers, embassy staff, international business executives, foreign investors, ex-pats returning home – in fact, anyone who is busy and may not live in the area they wish to move to. How will you access these markets? Contact embassies and personnel departments in large multi-nationals; consider advertising in in-flight magazines and international papers like the *European*. You have lots of benefits to help you sell the service. Make sure you spell them out. Ask your solicitor to draw up an agreement for you to use with clients which clearly sets out the scope of your work, your liabilities and agreed fees.

Moving house is time-consuming. Your personalised service could solve the problem for a lot of people who would happily pay for the very real help it brings.

This will appeal if

- You have good interpersonal skills.
- You're good at assessing properties.
- You enjoy travel.
- You have some knowledge of buying procedures.
- You're good at understanding people's needs.

Advantages

- Low overheads.
- Low cost start-up.
- Potentially lucrative business.

Disadvantages

- Advertising costs can be high.
- Delay in payment affects cash flow.
- Could involve abortive efforts.

Future possibilities

- Extend business to include full range of property and legal services, including removals and visa applications.
- Establish a business property finding service.
- Establish offices in major European cities.

Way 76 Property maintenance

Landlords, shops, businesses, elderly people, busy executives and all non-practical householders are potential customers for a property maintenance service. If you have good, practical skills this could be the business for you.

The level of maintenance you are able to offer will be dictated, to some extent, by your own particular skills. However, having said that, you can always sub-contract work to other professionals, taking a percentage commission instead. Spend some time finding reliable plumbers, decorators, electricians, builders and other professionals whom you could call on and who would provide the high quality of service you require.

You could operate on a contract basis with your customers, agreeing on a list of jobs to do on a regular basis: checking drains, leaf clearance, window cleaning, cleaning communal parts in flats and so on. It could also cover a set number of call-outs, too. The other way of operating is through the less lucrative call-out only service.

To find your customers, place adverts in local magazines and papers, and do leaflet drops to households. Try negotiating a deal with property letting agencies who could pass on your details to landlords, and in exchange earn themselves a commission.

'Cowboys' have made people wary of manual workers. Help reassure them by looking professional – and acting that way too. A simple overall uniform printed with your business name will help to reinforce the right image, as will letter-headed notepaper and proper invoices. But at the end of the day it will be the quality of service which will help to enhance your reputation and turn your business into an enterprising success.

This will appeal if

- You enjoy practical work and have some basic repair skills.
- You like variety.
- You're organised and efficient.
- You're trustworthy.

Advantages

- Contract work assures a regular income and work flow.
- Low running costs.

- Varied work.
- Good market potential.

Disadvantages

- Some investment in equipment and transport needed.
- Earnings are somewhat limited by the number of hours you can work.

Future possibilities

- Expand range of skills and services through additional staff.
- Tender for larger commercial contracts.
- Establish operations in other areas.
- Establish and develop separate operations: decorating, plumbing, building etc.

Address

Cleaning and Support Services Association, Suite 73–74, The Hop Exchange, 24 Southwark Street, London SE1 1TY; 0171-403 2747

Way 77 Publishers' remainders

Not every book becomes a bestseller. So what are publishers to do with all those unsold copies when it costs money to warehouse them? They could pulp them or, even better, sell them to a remainder agent who buys the books cheaply and sells them on again to … yourself?

You have the opportunity to pick up books – hardback and paperback – at ridiculously low prices. As a result you are able to offer them to the book-hungry public at much cheaper prices than when they first appeared in the high street. And everyone loves a bargain.

How you sell them is the next thing to consider. Study your locality. Would a market stall be the best place, or a shop, or could you sell them through house parties, or even school staff rooms?

Similarly, your potential market will dictate the type of books you buy. In this business it may not necessarily be a good idea to specialise. Look at the local bookshops – your main competitors.

Decide if you should try to compete with them by offering a similar choice of books or offer a completely different selection.

Where do you buy your stock? From book remainder agents. These are the people who buy the remaindered titles direct from the publishers and are listed in the *Directory of Publishing*, Volume 1 (see below). There are some 40 or so in the UK, so there should be one near you.

This will appeal if

- You positively enjoy books.
- You're reasonably fit – books are very heavy.
- You have a knowledge of the book trade.

Advantages

- Good mark-up.
- Cheaper prices for customers mean that impulse buying is more likely.
- Everyone loves a bargain.

Disadvantages

- May need transport.
- What do you do with *your* unsold stock?
- It's a gamble that anyone will want to buy a book from you which the publishers themselves couldn't shift!

Future possibilities

- If you start with a market stall, acquire shop premises.
- Open outlets in other towns and begin to develop your business identity.
- Move into mainstream book retailing.
- Develop second-hand book sales.
- Become a remainder agent yourself.

Publication

Directory of Publishing, Volume 1 (UK), by the Publishers' Association; Cassell (annual)

Lists publishers and remainder agents.

Way 78 Reconditioning equipment

Most people tend to think of dustbin refuse when you mention 'recycling', but household equipment can also be recycled and form the basis for a successful, and ecologically attractive, enterprising business.

Finding the equipment to work on should present few difficulties. Most people are only too eager to have someone take old machines off their hands. Stereos, washing machines, toasters, televisions, fridges – in fact, any household appliance could be recycled. Think about the possibility of specialising in just one type: stereos or fridges or items from the 1950s. This would make it easier to market yourself and find essential suppliers of spare parts.

Think about the skills you have to offer. The more work you can do yourself, the better, but it is vitally important that you know what you are doing. The law is strict about the sale of electrical goods so if you're not a qualified electrician, think of recruiting a partner who is or build the cost of farming the work out into your prices. Your forte might be the decorative aspect instead. Revamping the exterior of a rusty old fridge can turn it into a trendy up-market object, attracting a high premium.

Space is essential both for work and storage of stock. Keep the working parts of equipment which is otherwise totally beyond repair. Use good bodywork to rescue a less attractive but working model. Manufacturers may help in tracing spare parts for old machines and scrap merchants could be useful too. Failing that, you can occasionally replace workings with modern counterparts.

Think about how you will sell your renovated stock. You could sell from your workshop, getting yourself known through advertising in local papers, or you could sell to retail outlets, particularly if you're aiming at the 'trendy' market.

Offering a guarantee would be a good selling point. But if your work is done well and to high standards, that alone should ensure the success of one of the few businesses which also contributes to the expanding 'green' movement.

This will appeal if

- You have high mechanical/technical abilities.

- You enjoy practical work.
- You have a good eye for design potential in objects.
- You enjoy fixing things.

Advantages

- Good potential mark-up on sales.
- Good access to stock.
- Good potential market for finished products.

Disadvantages

- Requires transport and workspace.
- Labour intensive work, but this is offset by the low cost of stock.
- Some investment in tools needed.

Future possibilities

- Acquire retail premises.
- Move into the collectors' market of objects like juke boxes and pinball machines.
- Hire additional expertise to develop other areas, eg reconditioning office equipment, photographic equipment, mechanical toys and clocks.

Address

Domestic Appliance Services Association, Hazeldene, Wengeo Lane, Ware, Herts SG12 0EG; 01920 465928

Publication
Kompass UK (monthly)
A directory of manufacturers' products and services.

Way 79 Recording studio

Setting up a recording studio is a large investment project but if you can make it work the rewards can be equally big.

Money first. Assuming you don't have access to the funds your market research has shown you will need, you could, armed with a well-developed business plan, approach investment companies. There is also the possibility of finding financial support from people you know, the contacts you have, or the community in which you live. People hold tightly on to their money and you will need to be able to reassure them with lots of facts and figures that their investment would be safe. Could you do that?

Your market research should reveal what the competition is like. Price may not be the one and only thing you have to compete on. What do the others offer? Could you better it? What do your potential customers want from a studio? Could you supply it? You may be surprised that what is wanted is unrelated to recording and something like improved refreshment facilities, easy access to banks and shops, or good links with a taxi service.

Decide if you want to target a particular sector of the recording market. Your research should help you work out if this would be a profitable option to consider or not.

Drawing up business plans and cash flow projections is important in order to validate any new business proposition. Obviously it is even more important when large amounts of money are involved. But if you can show that this is a realistic proposition based on thorough research you should have no problem in finding investors with the money to fund your enterprise.

This will appeal if

- You have good PR skills.
- You have some relevant knowledge or experience.
- You have access to funds or feel competent about your abilities to raise them.
- You have some business experience and expertise.

Advantages

- With regular work, potential earnings are high.
- Strong likelihood of repeat business.

Disadvantages

- High investment costs.
- Intermittent work flow at first.

Future possibilities

- Expand premises and improve facilities to respond to increased work flow.
- Expand into video production.
- Diversify into public address and audio-visual equipment hire.

Addresses

Association of Professional Recording Services, 2 Windsor Square, Silver Street, Reading, Berks RG1 2TH; 0118 975 6218

British Venture Capital Association, Essex House, 12–13 Essex Street, London WC2R 3AA; 0171-240 3846

Publication
Studio Sound (monthly)

Way 80 Renovating junk furniture

Renovating junk furniture is quite different from the highly specialised restoration work carried out on antiques. There the emphasis is on retaining the original features and restoring them to their former glory. With junk furniture it's not.

After finding stock from house clearances (advertise in local papers), auctions, jumble sales, car boot sales or even skips, the possibilities of what you can do with each piece are enormous. Do a straightforward repolish, strip down to bare wood, paint, varnish, stencil, add legs on or take them off, remove modern handles, put on old ones. Stipple, apply gold leaf or add a marble surface. The only limits to what you can do are your practical abilities, time, and your imagination.

You could decide to specialise: in chairs, tables, pine furniture, 1950s' furniture or renovations using original crafts. Your own artistic design could become a specialism in itself, in which case try to get some of the glossies to do a feature on your work – in fact, try to get them to do a feature anyway.

You could sell your finished products from your own workshop by advertising in local papers or house and home magazines. You could sell to up-market retail shops whose stock reflects the style you produce. You could also send photographs of your work to interior designers or invite them along to have a look at the sort of work you handle – entice them with a glass of wine or two. Once you become known for your work and high standards you should find customers coming to you instead.

For someone with a fertile imagination and a range of practical skills, renovating junk furniture could lead the way to a special niche in the market place.

This will appeal if

- You're practical.
- You have a good eye for design.
- You're creative.
- You enjoy fixing things.
- You're good at seeing the potential in objects.

Advantages

- Cost of stock very low.
- Good mark-up on finished products.
- Job satisfaction.
- Varied work.
- Could start in your spare time.

Disadvantages

- Requires work space, storage and transport.
- Some investment in tools and equipment needed.
- Labour intensive.

Future possibilities

- Acquire retail premises.
- Produce original designs.
- Have popular items mass produced.
- Expand into antique restoration.

Publication

Doing Up Old Junk, Joanna Jones; Merehurst, 1994

Way 81 Re-upholstering

Fortunately for you, new settees, chairs and suites can be expensive, so people frequently re-cover worn-looking upholstery instead. However, this is not a job for the faint-hearted and if you're adept with the sewing machine you could find yourself with a stream of customers only too willing to pay someone else to do it for them.

Market research the competition. What is the quality of their work and service like? Perhaps they only do loose covers and you see an opportunity to offer permanent ones. They may have a relatively slow turnround time and you know you could do pieces in half the time. Perhaps they have not thought about customer care and leave people with nothing to sit on while the work is being done. You could offer a basic replacement suite, perhaps with a choice of loose covers to suit different decor. Offering a guarantee with your work is also a good selling point. Competitive pricing will obviously help, too.

Once your reputation becomes established, work should come by word of mouth. But initially you could advertise in local and county papers, house and home magazines. You could also approach antique dealers, interior designers and fabric shops (which don't offer this service) and enter into commission agreements with them.

Re-upholstering offers lots of opportunities to establish yourself in business. If you have the necessary skills, it could be for you.

This will appeal if

- You have good sewing skills.
- You have an eye for detail.
- You're reliable.
- You're reasonably fit – or have access to some strong bodies to help collect and deliver work.

Advantages

- Good market potential.
- Good cash flow set-up.
- Can start in your spare time.
- May already have necessary equipment.

Disadvantages

- Experience needed.
- Transport and work space needed.
- Requires investment in tools and sewing machine.

Future possibilities

- Extend the range of services: re-caning, upholstery cleaning, cushion making, curtain making.
- If not already doing so, investigate the antiques market.
- Re-upholster bought chairs and sell on to retail outlets.
- Acquire shop premises, selling fabric, re-upholstered furniture, and of course your service.
- Establish outlets/operations in other areas.

Address

Guild of Master Craftsmen, 166 High Street, Lewes, East Sussex, BN7 1XU; 01273 478449

Way 82 Running a playgroup

Pre-school facilities are more in demand now than before. You can turn this to your advantage and establish a playgroup.

There are different levels at which you can operate. As a home-based childminder you are limited in the number you can take care of to two or three children, but with appropriate premises you could establish a larger group. This will obviously cost more, but you will also have more money coming in. Do some careful costings and cash flow projections. One thing which you will be able to project is income since it is likely that all available places will be readily snapped up.

There are, however, prerequisites. You must be registered with your local Social Services Department which vets applications. Your credentials are important. You will need some relevant experience, perhaps in nursing, education or child care.

One enterprising establishment in London decided to market the 'alternative' slant and prepares only natural wholefoods at mealtimes. This sort of unique selling point (USP) could attract a much higher premium. Market research should reveal whether this would find enough uptake in your area.

Child care can be incredibly hard work. However, it is one area in which the demand often outweighs supply. Unlike other businesses you will probably have no difficulty finding customers. And with thorough groundwork and financial planning you could supply a much needed service.

This will appeal if

- You love children – all the time.
- You have some relevant experience, including first aid.
- You're reasonably fit.
- You're a good manager.

Advantages

- Strong market demand.
- Good cash flow set-up.
- Low overheads if operating as a childminder at home.

Disadvantages

- Overheads of premises.
- Requires investment in toys and facilities.
- Very demanding work.
- Being a childminder ties you to the home.

Future possibilities

- Move into larger premises.
- Establish additional playgroups to meet demand.
- Establish playgroups in other locations.
- Establish a preparatory school.

Addresses

National Childminding Association, 8 Masons Hill, Bromley, Kent BR2 9EY; 0181-464 6164

Pre-School Learning Alliance, 69 Kings Cross Road, London WC1X 9LL; 0171-833 0991

Publications
Childcare Business (bi-monthly)
Nursery World (weekly)
Starting a Playgroup; Pre-School Learning Alliance, 1991

Way 83 Secondhand goods

Recycling other people's unwanted items is a concept as old as the hills, but can still provide the sound foundation for a business today.

Books: Secondhand books hold a fascination for many book lovers, providing a constant, ready-made market. You might become a 'runner', which means buying large quantities of books at auction or through house clearances and selling them on as job lots to shops. You could supply dealers with individual books (Way 6), or you might decide to run your own market stall or shop.

Clothes: We're not talking here about smelly cast-offs which no one wants. We are talking about re-cycling good quality, collectable, even designer label items. Children's clothes could prove popular, especially since new ones are so expensive and children grow out of them incredibly quickly. There is also a market in supplying film, television and theatre companies. Let them know about your type of stock.

Find new stock at house clearances (advertise in local papers), auctions (buy *Antiques Trade Gazette*), from jumble or car boot sales. Do any running repairs and alterations, clean and press the clothes, and put them on good hangers. Include all these costs in the price. It may help sales to stress to customers that the clothes have already been laundered or dry cleaned.

Records/cassettes/CDs/videos/computer software: In West London a highly successful business started many years ago in this field and is still going strong after several expansions, but besides just *selling* items they also offer a part-exchange option as well. It does require some knowledge of working in the music field, not only to be able to give an excellent service, but also to be able to spot valuable collectors' items when they come in.

Although you may be dealing in secondhand goods, there is no reason why you should not create your own strong business image. Reinforce it through printed bags, advertising and even printed T-shirts and sweatshirts. Get your name and reputation known for giving a good service and you should find your customers returning time and again.

This will appeal if

- You're organised.
- You have some knowledge of the type of items you sell.
- You are enthusiastic about your stock.
- You are reasonably fit.

Advantages

- Good mark-up on stock.
- Can start in your spare time.
- Lots of repeat business.

Disadvantages

- Some investment in stock needed.
- Requires transport and storage if you're running a market stall.

Future possibilities

- Acquire shop premises if you start with a market stall.
- Open outlets in other locations.
- Diversify: Way 78; Way 80; Way 81.
- Trade upmarket, attending auctions etc.
- Investigate trading via the Internet (Way 44).

Publications

For useful addresses and publications for secondhand books see Way 6.
Record Collector (monthly)

Way 84 Security work

Being burgled appears to be a common hazard of everyday life, especially in bigger cities. However, your business could help people to prevent crime by improving basic security around their homes – before a break-in ever happens.

It requires in-depth knowledge of a wide range of security devices: window and door locks, door reinforcements, lighting, smoke alarms and security marking. Contact manufacturers for full details of their product ranges. Unless you are experienced, leave burglar alarms to the professionals and earn yourself a commission by introducing clients to them instead.

With good DIY skills you should be able to install the majority of smaller fittings although there are some, such as hinge bolts, which may need someone more skilled. This is where a partnership could help; otherwise, sub-contract, but make sure of the quality of the work since it will reflect on you.

Local police stations have their own crime prevention officers. Arrange a meeting to explain about your business. The police handle many enquiries from the public and provide the names of local security businesses on request – a good way for you to acquire work.

Other customers can be found by advertising through local papers which you should also watch for reports of burglaries and break-ins. While people's awareness is raised you could leaflet drop households in the surrounding area.

Setting up this business requires a fair bit of groundwork beforehand, but armed with the right knowledge and a good business plan your enterprise should be as secure as your clients' houses.

This will appeal if

- You have good interpersonal skills.
- You have some selling skills – or are willing to learn.
- You're practical.

Advantages

- Low cost start-up.
- As an independent adviser you have more credibility than a salesperson representing only one company's products.
- Low overheads.
- Good cash flow set-up.

Disadvantages

- No repeat business.

- Delay in commission payments from alarm companies.
- People may take your advice but fit devices themselves.

Future possibilities

- Hire additional staff to cover wider areas.
- Extend the service to other security work, eg photographing valuables.
- Run classes in personal safety.
- Franchise the operation.
- Develop and market your own range of security devices.

Address

Master Locksmiths' Association, Units 4 and 5, Business Park, Woodford Halse, Daventry, Northants NN11 3PZ; 01327 262255

Publications
Security Installer (monthly)
Security Specifier Magazine (bi-monthly)
Securitech (annual)
The Complete Guide to Home Security, David Alan Wacker; Betterway Publications Inc, 1990
Handbook of Business Security, Keith Hearnden and Alec Moore; Kogan Page, 1996
Home Security, Sonia Aarons and Donna Gilbert; Haynes, 1995

Way 85 Sell your knowledge

We all tend to undervalue our abilities, aptitudes, skills, experience and knowledge instead of capitalising on them. You could be using yours to form the basis of a new enterprise.

Spend some time making a list of as many things as possible that you can do or know about. Really brainstorm and don't limit yourself to things connected with your last or present job, although this may be a good place to start. For example, if you have been a secretary you will know how to set up and maintain filing systems, organise office procedures, arrange office catering and use word processors.

Think about your hobbies, any collections you may have,

domestic skills, craft skills. What have you done a lot of in your life? Have you organised charity events? What do people always compliment you on and what do they always ask you about rather than anyone else? Your answers are valuable. See them as possibly holding germs of business ideas instead of just taking them for granted or relegating them to your CV.

The most obvious way to use what you know is as a consultant (see Way 53). Depending on what your forte is, you may find you have the necessary skills to offer an advisory service, help new businesses, be a troubleshooter or become a temporary worker to cover absences. You could also write books or articles drawing on your past experience or up-to-date knowledge (see Way 101). Or what about running classes (Way 95) or training sessions (Way 93)?

Brainstorm as many ideas on how to use your skills as you can. Then do your market research, draw up your business plan and cash flow projections, and see your wealth of experience turn into wealth of a different kind.

These suggestions will all depend on you as an individual, but very broadly:-

This will appeal if

- You're confident about your knowledge/abilities etc.
- You have good interpersonal skills.
- You're enthusiastic.

Advantages

- Potential earnings high – people are willing to pay for expertise.
- Low investment – you've already invested your time to reach this level.

Disadvantage

- May have to pick up some business skills first to turn your ideas into a going concern.

Future possibilities

- As your reputation becomes known it will be easier to find work.

- Be more selective about the commissions you accept.
- Raise your fees to help control increased work flow. However, this can also have the effect of increasing your perceived value and therefore the demand for your services.

Publication
Sell Your Knowledge, Monica Nicou, Christine Ribbing and Eva Ading; Kogan Page, 1994

Way 86 Speciality foods

Dounne Alexander-Moore finally decided to leave her husband. As a single parent, the problem was how to cope. An old recipe for hot chilli sauce came to mind and her flourishing business now supplies Harrods.

Wine bars, delicatessens, health food shops and specialist food shops are all potential customers for food specialities. Think about a particularly successful recipe of yours: a relish, a pastry, a curry, pies, patés, chocolates, pasta – almost anything uniquely home-made. Remember that fresh foods will mean cooking or baking every day, leaving you little time to find new customers, while packaged foods can be made in bulk but tend to be slower selling items. Think carefully about which would be best for you.

When you have decided, make up some samples and try them out at some likely shops. Note the shops' reactions and comments and be prepared to answer searching questions about how you make it, the ingredients, delivery times etc. You also need to find what price the shops would be willing to pay. Don't ask them for a price – suggest one and see what they say. They may want to do a sale or return first order.

Before you go into production, apply for a food-handling licence from your local Environmental Health Officer. You will also have to decide if you need to organise special packaging (can be expensive) and transport for delivery.

But once you have these organised a food business of this sort holds many possibilities for the competent cook.

This will appeal if

- You enjoy cooking/baking.
- You're methodical and organised.
- You have some basic selling skills – or are willing to acquire them.

Advantages

- Potentially huge market.
- The food trade is relatively stable.
- The business can be started in your spare time.

Disadvantages

- Some start-up costs.
- Packaging can be costly.

Future possibilities

- Invest in commercial preparation equipment.
- Acquire premises to meet increases in demand.
- Expand the customer base nationwide.
- Supply supermarket chains.
- Sell to Europe.
- Extend the range of products.

Address

Cookery and Food Association, 1 Victoria Parade, by 331 Sandycombe Road, Richmond, Surrey TW9 3NB; 0181-948 3870

Way 87 Surplus stock

Dealing in surplus stock is, I think, a business for the true entrepreneur. If you're shrewd and quick-thinking this could be the business for you.

Firstly, find out from manufacturers and businesses what surplus stock they have. It might be the result of over-ordering, end of lines, bankrupt stock or stock which is simply redundant for their purposes. Tell them you may be willing to take it off their hands and if you're clever you could get the stock for a pittance

– they'll just be glad not to have to pay any more storage costs. However, don't give them a firm commitment to buy yet.

Next, find out how much the stock would normally be worth to a buyer. It should exceed what you pay for it by a significant amount. Then contact potential buyers, offering the stock at a discount price but one which still provides a significant profit for yourself. Once you have a customer, confirm the purchase with your supplier. And if you're very clever you could try to get payment from your buyer up-front, and 30 days' credit from your supplier. This will give you additional money for a month in which to finance other deals.

You could maximise sales by sending out a regular bulletin to potential buyers, listing surplus stock which you have located.

With low overheads and speedy turnover of stock this could be the profitable business idea you have been looking for.

This will appeal if

- You're good at spotting opportunities.
- You're fast-acting.
- You have some selling skills – or are willing to acquire them.
- You have good interpersonal skills.
- You have good telephone skills.

Advantages

- Good mark-up on stock.
- Low risk business (you don't buy until you have a customer).
- No storage space needed.
- Good cash flow set-up.

Disadvantages

- Requires transport.
- Irregular work flow to start.

Future possibilities

- Continued expansion of opportunities as contacts grow.
- You could decide to specialise and establish a regular wholesaling business in a particular area.
- Importing (see Way 42) and exporting has possibilities too.

Publications
Kompass UK (annual)
A directory of manufacturers' products and services.
Sell's Directory of Products and Services (annual)

Way 88 Telecottages

Being in at the start when new trends emerge can be one of the best ways to start a successful enterprise. One such trend is for people to work remotely from their normal place of work, using telecommunications to link either to their employer's office or to clients, customers and other businesses. This is known as *teleworking*. Teleworkers may be employed or self-employed.

Although many who have switched to this way of working use their own home as the base from which they work, this does have its drawbacks and does not suit everyone. Lack of space, peace and quiet, equipment, and opportunities to socialise with others, can mean that working at home proves impractical for some, and an unattractive proposition for others.

To bridge this gap are *telecottages*. These are fully equipped office spaces which cater to the needs of teleworkers who pay to use the facilities, much like hiring ordinary office space. Not only do telecottages provide access to equipment, but they also overcome the potential problem of isolation which can affect people who work alone.

Set up costs for telecottages are high, but grants may be available in your location. Anything which will bring employment to an area or help promote it as a 'virtual' business centre is in a strong position to attract seed capital from government and other sources. For example, Highlands and Islands Enterprise in Scotland has helped with initial funding for one such telecottage, along with BT and the local council. You may wish to consider approaching employers with a proposal to run a telecottage for their employees.

As working patterns change, daily commuting becomes less and less attractive, and employers look for new ways to cut overheads of employing staff in-house, setting up and running a telecottage could be where your new future begins.

This will appeal if

- You are organised with good office or premises management skills.
- You have sound marketing and networking skills.
- You have some understanding of telecommunications and their applications, although being an expert is not necessary.
- You enjoy working with people.

Advantages

- Grants and commercial backing or sponsorship may be available to help with start up and running costs.
- Teleworking is an emerging trend which looks set to expand.
- No more city living or commuting.
- Inexpensive locations compared with the premium rates in city centres.
- Can be set up and run as a co-operative.

Disadvantages

- As a new concept, heavy promotion may be required in the initial stages.
- High start up costs if grants not available.

Future possibilities

- Establish other telecottages in other locations.
- Franchise the operation.
- Negotiate with employers to set up and operate a nationwide string of telecottages on their behalf.
- Once established, install a manager to handle the day-to-day running while you develop other business ideas.

Addresses

Industrial Common Ownership Movement, Vassalli House, 20 Central Road, Leeds LS1 6DE; 0113 246 1737/8. Your first point of contact if you are interested in setting up a co-operative business.

Telework, Telecottage and Telecentre Association (TCA), WREN Telecottage, Stoneleigh Park, Warwickshire CV8 2RR; 01203 696986. Compuserve 100114,2366.
http://ourworld.compuserve.com/homepages/Teleworker/
Compuserve Forum: GO TWEURO

Publications
Teleworker (bi-monthly)
New Work Options, Christine Ingham; Thorsons, 1996
The Teleworking Handbook; TCA

Way 89 Teleworking

Teleworking is not so much a business as a way of working; one which can open the door to self-employment – one which may have previously remained firmly closed simply because of where you live. Until this innovation it has been vitally important for businesses to be located where their customers are, so for those in remote locations or unemployment black spots, setting up in business has been difficult; but as teleworkers will tell you in the Highlands of Scotland (dubbed the teleworking capital of Europe), location becomes unimportant when you start teleworking.

What teleworking means is working in a 'remote' location, using telecommunications technology to connect with customers, clients, suppliers and other businesses in order to conduct your business. So instead of arranging a person-to-person meeting with a new client and their team to discuss the progress of a project, a video-conference brings everyone together in face-to-face virtual contact instead. Work, commissions and negotiations are all transmitted on-line, by electronic mail, fax or phone – and occasionally by what has now come to be known as 'snail mail', ie post. Advances in technology now make some businesses' geographical locations unimportant – Hong Kong harbour's dock traffic is controlled by a teleworker in Orkney; another on-line teleworker there solves problems for oil companies in the Middle East.

Think about how your business idea might be adapted. Read Way 44, Internet businesses and Way 88, Telecottages. What may previously have been seen as an insurmountable obstacle to becoming self-employed, ie your location, may turn out to be no problem at all by adapting your idea to teleworking.

This will appeal if

- Your location has previously been a hindrance to becoming self-employed.

- Your business does not depend (and few do) on actual physical contact, eg massage or osteopathy.
- You are comfortable with new technology, or are willing to learn.

Advantages

- Location is unimportant.
- Gives access to a global market instead of relying on just the local or even national market.
- Low running costs.
- Read Way 44 and Way 88.

Disadvantages

- Investment in equipment required.
- Isolation can be a problem.

Future possibilities

- Depends on the business you establish.
- Join a telecottage if isolation becomes a problem.
- Set up and run a telecottage, if none already exists in your own locality. See Way 88.

Addresses

See Way 88.
National Association of Teleworkers, The Island House, Midsomer Norton, Bath, Avon BA3 2HL; 01761 413869.

Publications
See Way 88.

Way 90 Themed cafés

Running a café is a popular idea with many wanting to run their own business. For some, the choice of style is low-key with a simple checkered tablecloth and traditional fare. But it is worth considering whether the location might warrant a more distinct design to provide a more unique, entertaining and attractive venue.

Keeping an eye on current and emerging trends is the best way to decide on the most appropriate, and potentially successful, theme. Finding out what has succeeded in other towns, cities and even countries could provide a clue to what might work for you – although one should be careful here. What might appeal to one cultural group may go down like a dead duck elsewhere. However, it seems that most things American cross the Atlantic successfully, so the States may provide some useful ideas.

Some current trends for themed cafés include: cybercafés – with computers linked to the Internet for customers to use while sipping a hot cappucino; fashion-themed cafés, complete with original designs on display and guest appearances; Hollywood; popular music; famous person/people. Others might include American retro, Bauhaus, art deco, Boswell-type coffee houses, or ones with art, literary or even a scientific theme.

Although the decor provides for good novelty value, the quality of food and service is still of paramount importance if the business is to survive in the long term. Your aim is to have customers returning time after time to sample once more the delicious range of coffees, meals, snacks and cakes to die for, rather than to have them popping in and leaving, never to return, after having satisfied their curiosity.

This will appeal if

- You have some experience of catering.
- You are inventive, with a commercially-minded approach.
- You are looking for ways in which to take the edge on the competition.
- You are good at PR.

Advantages

- The novelty value makes PR easy, bringing it to the forefront of the public's awareness.
- A top quality themed café which can attract a good turnover of customers lends itself to prime locations.
- Depending on the theme, may make it easier to target advertisements to reach potential customers.
- The theme element makes it easier to capture customers who might otherwise be difficult to attract.

Disadvantages

- Novelty value may have limited life span.
- May involve higher than normal start-up costs.
- What works in central London may have difficulty sustaining itself in a small town.
- Some otherwise potential customers may find a chosen theme off-putting.

Future possibilities

- Develop a programme of special occasions, eg guest appearances, special displays, fundraising events for local charities.
- Develop a line of related merchandise.
- Develop other related and marketable activities.
- Obtain a licence to serve alcohol.
- Open cafés in other locations.
- Consider franchising the operation.

Addresses and publications
See Way 16.

Way 91 Toy making

Cheap plastic toys are the norm today. However, this means there could now be a gap in the market for handmade toys made from natural materials. You won't be able to compete on price but you will be able to compete on quality and originality.

Although toys are for children it is adults who buy them. Capitalise on this and stress the ecological benefits of your non-plastic products, and that any wood you use is from sustainable sources.

You may choose to replicate original designs (check the patents) in which case your toys could have a nostalgic appeal to adults as well, broadening the potential market even more. On the other hand you may decide to originate some totally new designs instead. Test them out on some children and see what their reactions are. Modify them if you need to.

Whichever way you choose, check with Trading Standards about the rules and regulations for making toys, and the materials you can and cannot use. Armed with that knowledge make up samples ready to take around to suitable toy and/or craft retail outlets. Toy museums may be interested in your work as well (and give you ideas for designs), or you may decide to sell the toys yourself at a local market or craft fair.

Decide if you will mass-produce successful designs or stick to original one-offs. Your cash flow projections should indicate which would be best.

Making toys can be rewarding in itself, and if you have good practical skills you could begin to see more tangible results from your work, too.

This will appeal if

- You have good practical skills.
- You have an eye for design.
- You have a good eye for detail.
- You're a quick worker.
- You're safety conscious.

Advantages

- You can try out samples beforehand.
- Good cash flow if you run a market stall.
- Satisfying work.
- You're able to capitalise on existing skills.

Disadvantages

- Some investment in tools and materials needed.
- Unit costs may price you out of the market.
- Requires workspace.

Future possibilities

- Use outworkers (if appropriate) to respond to demand.
- Develop other ranges, eg household products.
- If not doing so, mass-produce popular lines.
- Expand customer base: consider export possibilities.
- Run craft-based workshops.

Addresses

British Toymakers Guild, 124 Walcot Street, Bath, Avon BA1 5BG; 01225 442440

British Toy and Hobby Manufacturers' Association, 80 Camberwell Road, London SE5 0EG; 0171-701 7271

Publications
Toy Trader (monthly)
Simple Wooden Toys, Ron Fuller and Cathy Meens; Headline, 1995
How to Make Moving Wooden Toys, Peter Holland; Cassell, 1995
Designing and Making Wooden Toys, Terry Kelly; Guild of Master Craftsmen, 1996
Making Wooden Toys and Games, Jeff Loader and Jennie Loader; Guild of Master Craftsmen, 1995

Way 92 Tracing family trees

Tracing people's family trees can be a fascinating business. However, you really do need to know what you're doing and the competition is fierce – so be warned.

This could be a business which you start in your spare time to allow you to gain as much experience of using different records and sources as possible. There are training courses which you may wish to consider and the Association of Genealogists and Record Agents operates an associate membership scheme which gives help while you're gaining experience.

With lots of competition you will have to think carefully about how you can take the edge. It could be by specialising: targeting the American market; working in a specific locality; targeting well-known local dignitaries. Your specialism could also be in how you present your findings. You could produce a video family tree, or present the information as a leather bound document or a framed 'tree' scroll. Offering to mail existing relatives with information about the successful findings could also lead to additional revenue from orders of copies.

The work can be an involved, lengthy process. Keep clients informed of progress at regular intervals to help them feel involved and to reassure them that you are providing a quality service.

It may be that you decide to operate the business in a part-time capacity to generate a second income. But if you enjoy research, address yourself to the competition and make yours a service with the edge, you could find yourself at the top of a different sort of tree.

This will appeal if

- You enjoy research and have good research skills.
- You're good at presenting written reports.
- You're tenacious.

Advantages

- Low overheads.
- Low investment.
- Fascinating work.

Disadvantages

- Intermittent work flow.
- Needs experience.
- Lots of competition.
- Can be frustrating.

Future possibilities

- Develop a mail order service for coat of arms products: wall plaques, engraved goblets, paper weights and so on.
- Diversify into company histories.

Address

Society of Genealogists, 14 Charterhouse Buildings, Goswell Road, London EC1M 7BA; 0171-251 8799. Organises classes and produces a quarterly publication, *Genealogists' Magazine.*

Publication
Family History (monthly)

Way 93 Training for businesses

Many large companies have departments whose sole brief is to train staff. This includes training new recruits; updating skills to facilitate promotion or movement within the company;

retraining to accommodate the introduction of new legislation, practices, reorganisations, technology or products; or to help managers work more effectively. The larger the company, the more varied the training needs. Inevitably there will be times when it is not possible to meet all training requirements without additional help. This is when independent trainers are called upon to supplement gaps in provision. (Smaller companies, not large enough to warrant a separate training department, also require trainers from time to time to deliver particular training programmes to their staff).

Experience of the field in which you aim to work is important. Being able to put on an entertaining show is not enough. Clients will be looking for good credentials and a demonstration of your understanding of their specific business sector or industry since each has its own distinct culture. Past contacts should provide the best starting point for developing a client list, with new ones coming through word of mouth.

The daily rate you charge needs to take into account that you will not be training every day throughout the year. A full schedule should involve no more than three days training a week. Office back-up will be needed to help you cope with administration and the preparation of materials for each new course, leaving you free to line up new contracts.

The world of work is constantly changing. Using your skills and experience to help others cope effectively with those changes can be a rewarding and lucrative step to take into the world of self-employment.

This will appeal if

- You have suitable experience and credentials.
- You are a good communicator.
- You enjoy working with people.
- You can communicate well with people at many different levels.
- You are both an analytical and innovative thinker.

Advantages

- Enables you to build on previous experience.
- Can be very well paid.

- Work can come by word of mouth.
- Can be satisfying work.

Disadvantages

- Overheads of employing administrative staff and office space, although this should be covered by your daily rate.
- May take some time to build up a client list.
- When businesses experience a down-turn, training budgets tend to be the first to go.
- Can be demanding work.

Future possibilities

- Join up with others who can supplement any training skills gaps you may have.
- Employ additional staff to deliver other training programmes.
- Develop 'off the peg' training packages to market to those companies who wish to deliver programmes in-house.
- Produce training videos.
- Investigate the possibility of delivering training via video-conferencing to remote or foreign locations.

Address

Institute of Personnel and Development, Camp Road, London SW19 4UX; 0181-971 9000.

Publications

Everything You Ever Needed to Know About Training, Kaye Thorne and David Mackey; Kogan Page, 1996
Training and Enterprise Directory; TEC National Council & Kogan Page. Annual.
How to Write and Prepare Training Materials, Nancy Stimson; IPD, 1991
Training Officer (monthly)
Management Training (quarterly)

Way 94 Translation work

With the UK at last becoming more Euro-orientated there are lots of opportunities if you have one or more foreign languages to offer.

You could accompany business people on visits and help them to negotiate deals. You could link in with their training programmes and offer business language tuition relevant to their particular field. You could also offer a written translation service of reports, manuals, advertising literature and sales material.

You may decide to target a particular business sector, becoming familiar with specialist terms and procedures, making contacts, and building up valuable in-depth international knowledge for which people will pay a high premium.

Potential businesses could be approached direct, either here or in the country in whose language you are proficient. Chambers of Commerce could also be approached. If you decide to advertise you could choose business magazines, trade journals or the business sections of the Sunday papers.

Look in Yellow Pages. You will find translation agencies listed through which you could find freelance work. And what about setting up your own agency?

Whichever way you decide to use your languages, do your market research thoroughly, and with proper planning you could find your specialist service in great demand.

This will appeal if

- You're fluent in at least one foreign language.
- You have some knowledge of, or interest in, business and commerce.
- You enjoy travel.
- You have a highly professional attitude.
- You have good interpersonal skills.

Advantages

- Opportunities to travel.
- Varied work.
- Low investment.
- Growing market awareness.

- Low overheads.
- High potential earnings.

Disadvantage

- Irregular work flow.

Future possibilities

- Acquire premises and employ additional translators with other languages.
- Run language courses.
- Establish operations in other cities.
- Develop and market commercial language materials and programmes.

Addresses

Translators' Association, Society of Authors, 84 Drayton Gardens, London SW10 9SB; 0171-373 6642. Advice on marketing, rates of pay, contracts. Specimen contract and information bulletin also available.

Institute of Translation and Interpreting, 377 City Road, London EC1V 1NA; 0171-713 7600

Publications

Language International (bi-monthly)
Translator's Handbook, Catriona Picken; Aslib, 1996

Way 95 Tuition

Do you have a specific skill, in-depth knowledge of a subject or a teaching qualification? Having expertise – academic or otherwise – can provide you with a marketable commodity. People will pay well to be shown 'How to ... play a Bach concerto, speak business French, read Tarot cards, or pass a GCSE'. Think carefully about the areas in which you are skilled and have experience. What do people ask your advice about? Perhaps you have a suitable background offering training in business or personal skills.

Tuition work is normally paid by the hour. Find out what the going rate is in your area – it could be anything from £5 to £50, depending on who you are and what sort of tuition you are offering.

Consider the possibility of running short courses for small (or large) groups. You could even run a residential course, booking the facilities of an attractive country hotel, local college, or six-berth cabin cruiser – depending on your course and clientele. You could also engage other specialists to make guest appearances.

Alternatively you could, instead of tutoring, become an agent who arranges work for others and takes a percentage of the fees.

Success will depend on your knowledge and abilities as a teacher, but being reliable, preparing well, being organised, and having a professional attitude are all important. Your aim is to build as good a reputation as you can. This will be its own advertisement and passport to success.

This will appeal if

- You enjoy working with people.
- You have a lot of patience.
- You're enthusiastic about your specialism.
- You're organised and reliable.

Advantages

- Being in a teaching environment without having to cope with the day-to-day hassle of working in a school or college.
- You can eventually choose which clients you take on.
- Low start-up costs.
- Some tuition work can be very lucrative.

Disadvantages

- Work can be intermittent at first.
- Seasonal fluctuations if your work is linked to term-time exams.
- Managing unrealistic parental pressure and expectations.
- Limited earnings in one-to-one work.

Future possibilities

- Increase fees in line with reputation.

- Establish a tutorial college.
- Extend the agency network beyond your immediate locality.
- Access foreign markets. Develop combined travel/study packages.

Address

Incorporated Association of Tutors, 63 King Edward Road, Northampton NN1 5LY

Publications
Freelance Teaching and Tutoring, John T Wilson; How To Books, 1996
Times Educational Supplement (weekly)

Way 96 Voluntary group

Over the years, the voluntary sector, consisting of registered charities and other not-for-profit organisations, has dramatically changed and expanded. The reasons don't concern us here, but what is of interest is that setting up a voluntary group can be one way of creating one's own employment while being of help to others too.

Setting up a voluntary group will not make you rich. If any profits are generated through the group's activities (and not all groups do, since many simply provide a free service) they are automatically ploughed back into the group's activities. However, it is perfectly acceptable to draw a salary for yourself and any others who play key roles in the successful running of the organisation.

As government and local council funding continues to be withdrawn from supporting many needy and vulnerable sectors of the community, opportunities arise for independent voluntary groups to meet that continuing need. Keep an eye on local, national and even international events. Changes and developments can often prompt the setting up of a new group, as can one's own personal experiences. The Suzy Lamplugh Trust is one such example, set up to raise the public's awareness of the need for personal safety after Suzy Lamplugh's mysterious disappearance. Opportunities may also exist to set up a local branch of an existing charity or voluntary group.

Although in previous years one tended to find mainly rich people involved in this sort of work, while lending their financial support to its activities, the picture has changed. Voluntary organisations can now look to the many trusts (including the national lottery), corporate coffers, private individuals, the general public, as well as their own fundraising activities to finance their venture. And despite the cut-backs, monies are still available for some projects from government, local and even EU sources.

If making a million is less of a priority than having a reasonable income while being able to contribute to making society a better place in which to live, setting up and running a voluntary group could be for you.

This will appeal if

- You are socially minded.
- You have a lot of drive and initiative.
- You are able to motivate others and fire them with your own enthusiasm for the project.
- You are organised and are good at planning.
- You are a good communicator.

Advantages

- It provides a way of creating your own employment (although this should not be your sole reason for setting up a group).
- You do not have to finance the venture out of your own pocket.
- You will be making a valuable contribution to society.

Disadvantages

- Fundraising can be hard work and time consuming.
- It may be difficult finding the volunteers.
- The competition for some funds can be quite fierce.

Future possibilities

This really does depend on the type of voluntary group you establish. Consider whether the group might:

- Expand into other localities.

- Go national if it started out on a local basis.
- Develop a commercial, income-generating division to help the group become self-financing.
- Offer a wider range of services and/or facilities for your client-user group.

Addresses

National Council for Voluntary Organisations, Regents Wharf, 8 All Saints Street, London N1 9RL; 0171-713 6161

Volunteer Centre UK, Carriage Row, 183 Eversholt Street, London NW1 1BU; 0171-388 9888

Publications
Voluntary Agencies Directory (annual)
Directory of Grant-making Trusts; Charities Aid Foundation. Available in most libraries.
How to Raise Funds and Sponsorship, Chriss McCallum; How to Books Ltd, 1992
Complete Fundraising Handbook; Directory of Social Change, 1993
How to Run a Voluntary Group, Chris Carling; How to Books Ltd, 1995
Charity Magazine (monthly)

Way 97 Wedding consultant

Every year approximately 350,000 couples marry, typically spending on average around £5000 for a white wedding. And anyone who has gone through the process of arranging one knows how traumatic and time-consuming it can be. As a wedding consultant you take the pressure off the bride and groom and become the person who organises everything from booking the wedding venue to arranging the reception and dance afterwards.

Being successful will depend greatly on your level of organisational skills; keeping your head when either bride, groom or one of their parents loses theirs; and on having good contacts. You will be liaising with a large number of different businesses and will need to be able to depend on the quality and reliability of their service. Having the right name and number to hand, plus a few back-ups, will make your job that much easier and help ensure you provide a high quality, professional service. Spending time beforehand to establish these contacts and build up your resource file is vital. With weddings there is no room for mistakes or second chances, which makes this a job where the adrenalin can really start to flow.

Make the service you offer as comprehensive as you feel comfortable with. For example, you may or may not want to go so far as to arrange honeymoons. But think about offering different levels of service, or special themed weddings like Victorian or 'rustic' ones.

Apart from the fee you charge to the couple, earnings can be boosted by negotiating with your suppliers discounts which you reserve, at least in part, to help cover your own costs.

Although there is unlikely to be much in the way of repeat business with this enterprise, if you become known for making that special day and all the preparations that go with it run smoothly and effortlessly, you should find one couple after another beating a speedy path to your door.

This will appeal if

- You are very well organised.
- You have good interpersonal skills.
- You are good at advising people when necessary.
- You can stay calm under pressure.
- You have lots of stamina.

Advantages

- Once established, work should come by word of mouth.
- As your resource list develops, organising each event should become easier.
- Two sources of income.
- Can be a very satisfying job.

Disadvantages

- No repeat business.
- It can be quite stressful.

- Some seasonality to the work: peak times in summer months with fewer in winter.
- Preparing to get married can be an emotional time – and you could find yourself caught in the crossfire.

Future possibilities

- Establish operations in other geographical areas.
- Franchise the operation.
- Open a one-stop wedding shop, for couples who are happy to organise their own weddings.

Publications
Brides & Setting up Home (bi-monthly)
Good Housekeeping's Wedding Magazine (quarterly)
Wedding and Home
Wedding Services Directory (annual)
Alternative Weddings, Jane Ross-MacDonald; Thorsons, 1996
Debrett's Wedding Guide, 1997
How to Plan a Wedding, Mary Kilborn; How To Books, 1995
Noble's Wedding Venues Guide; Noble Publishing, 1997

Way 98 Window boxes

Window boxes add character to any frontage whether domestic or commercial. You could use your green fingers to provide a specialist service which plants and maintains them.

You do need some knowledge about plants and window box planting. Some species are more suitable than others, and need different maintenance, drainage and positioning. Looking pretty isn't enough. If your experience has previously been with gardens, invest some time on research.

Market research should also reveal the likely uptake of the service and what the competition, if any, is like. If there is, what are their rental charges? What do the displays look like? Can you compete? If there isn't any competition, why not? Use all this information, together with your costings of supplies and overheads, to draw up your business plan and cash flow projections.

To launch your business you could offer to dress a centrally located business or shop for free. In exchange you receive 'free' advertising; the benefit to them is obvious. You could also use photographs of the display in your sales literature which you can then mail direct to other businesses, offering free quotes. And since you will be working outdoors don't forget that you can be your own advertisement by wearing a simple uniform printed with your business name and number.

Green-fingered skills and an eye for design are what's needed for this business. Back that up with a high quality service and you should enhance not only your customer's business but your own as well.

This will appeal if

- You're good with plants.
- You have a good eye for design.
- You're reasonably fit.
- You're reliable.

Advantages

- Good cash flow set-up from regular maintenance payments.
- Low overheads.
- Enjoyable work.
- Your service advertises itself.

Disadvantages

- Weather – working in it, and its effect on plants.
- Requires transport.
- Investment in stock required.
- Prior knowledge required.

Future possibilities

- Indoor office displays.
- Domestic patio design and planting.
- Synthetic plant arrangements.
- Hire additional staff to cover other areas, or franchise the operation.
- Acquire retail premises and benefit from passing trade.
- Establish your own nursery.

Publication
Creating Wonderful Window Boxes, Martin Baxendale; Ward Lock, 1994

There are lots of other useful books available. Check with your local library.

Way 99 Window cleaning

Window cleaning is one of the traditional areas for self-employment because it has the advantage of being a low cost start-up and it caters to a real need. Demand is always there.

As with many other businesses, you could consider taking the basic business concept and specialising. You could target factories, high security buildings like banks or jewellers, or specialise in cleaning shop signs or windows (or both). You could also target the domestic market or perhaps specialise in tall, multi-storey buildings.

Market research your ideas thoroughly. Find out about the competition and, if people are happy with the service, find out why. See if you can improve on it. And find out about health and safety regulations and insurance (see below).

Advertise in the areas where you wish to operate. Newsagents' windows and leaflet drops are both possibilities. Businesses can be approached direct. Be professional and wear a simple uniform printed with your name and number to advertise your service while you work. And once you have your round established in one area, move on to the next and drum up custom there. A lot of this work could come from personal recommendation.

Window cleaning illustrates that you don't have to re-invent the wheel to establish a new enterprise. This is a tried and tested business. Can you make it work for you?

This will appeal if

- You're reasonably fit.
- You enjoy working outdoors.
- You enjoy routine.
- You're reliable.

Advantages

- Regular work flow and income once customer base established.
- Low cost start-up.
- Good cash flow set-up.
- Low overheads.

Disadvantages

- Not much variety.
- Work affected by the weather.
- Transport necessary if your work involves the use of taller ladders.

Future possibilities

- Hire staff to cover additional areas.
- Offer additional services – door cleaning, brass plate cleaning, window frame painting.
- Develop full exterior decorating service.
- Offer window/door replacement service, acting as an agent on a commission fee basis.
- Expand into other exterior maintenance and repair work through sub-contracting.

Address

National Federation of Master Window Cleaners, Summerfield House, Harrogate Road, Reddish, Stockport, Cheshire SK5 6HQ; 0161-432 8754. Offers information about insurance and health and safety regulations.

Publication
Prevention of Falls to Window Cleaners; Health and Safety Executive, 1992

Way 100 Window dressing

Shop windows are important, which is why large department stores spend so much on window dressing – they appreciate the need to attract valuable customers.

While large high street stores have people qualified in art and design to dress their windows, the high fees involved put this outside the reach of smaller independent shops. If you have an eye for design and a flair for presentation you could offer a window dressing service to these smaller retail businesses.

Spend some time studying shop windows. Decide which are good displays and which are bad, those which never change and those which do but still look the same. Target the shops you think you could help. Sketch some ideas out beforehand and approach the shop in person, ready with your costings. You could even offer to do a shop window for free to launch your service. Perhaps, when other shop owners see your work (in person or in 'before and after' photographs) they will be impressed enough to want you to handle *their* window displays. From there, start to build a portfolio of your work. Keep an ideas file, too.

Remember that although your work will advertise itself you could also place a discreet business sticker in each window, and wearing a T-shirt printed with your business name advertises you while you work.

This business also lends itself to specialisation. For example, you could decide to dress only chemist shop windows and earn yourself a reputation in that field. If you can negotiate a contract with small chains of shops and give them the same identity, even better.

Competition is always tough for small shops. Your service could be just what they need to improve their image and increase profits for both of you.

This will appeal if

- You have a good eye for design.
- You have a fertile imagination.
- You're practical.
- You're good at communicating your ideas.

Advantages

- Regular work once customer base is established.
- Varied work.
- Your work advertises itself.
- Low overheads.

Disadvantages

- Requires transport.
- Requires artistic abilities.

Future possibilities

- Move up-market and handle larger accounts.
- Hire additional staff to respond to work flow.
- Negotiate a commission agreement with shop sign and retail design companies.

Way 101 Writing

There are many more opportunities in this field other than by writing block-buster novels. If writing appeals to you, start to broaden your outlook and spend time investigating just how many different sorts of writing there are. Here are a few: copy writing, writing business plans and reports, articles for journals and magazines, teenage magazine stories, greeting card verses, training materials, technical writing and writing fillers (crosswords, tips, anecdotes etc).

Look at your own interests, knowledge and experience to help you decide in which area/s to concentrate. For example, if you have spent a number of years in a personnel setting you could offer articles to appropriate business magazines, or present a synopsis for a book to suitable publishers. The *Writers' Handbook* and the *Writers' and Artists' Yearbook* are invaluable reference books and will help you work out who to approach.

There are also lots of books about writing: how to do it and how to make money out of it. Spend some time researching them in your library and decide which market to target.

Writing offers many opportunities (too many to go into in any depth here) but if you think it might be for you, consider the area you could specialise in, and use your library to help you discover possible openings. And like any other business venture, do your market research, draw up your business plans and cash flow projection and put that marketing plan into action.

This will appeal if

- You enjoy writing and have excellent writing skills.

- You're good at meeting deadlines.
- You're good at research.
- You're good at brief taking.
- You have some relevant knowledge/experience in your chosen area.

Advantages

- Low overheads.
- Low cost set-up.
- Can start in your spare time.
- Varied work.

Disadvantages

- Irregular work flow.
- Investment in a word processor would help.

Future possibilities

- Establish a writing agency.
- Progress into book-length manuscripts.
- Run writing courses on your specialist area.

Publications
Writers' and Artists' Yearbook; A & C Black, annual
Writer's Handbook; Macmillan, annual
Writers' Monthly

There are lots of books about the craft of writing and writing for particular markets. Some are listed in the above books; research others at your local library.

Useful Addresses

British Coal Enterprise Ltd, Business Funding, Edwinstowe House, Edwinstowe, Mansfield, Notts NG21 9PR; 0162 382 568. Help for businesses wishing to set up in a coalmining area.

British Steel Industry Ltd, Canterbury House, 2–6 Sydenham Road, Croydon CR9 2LJ; 0181-686 2311
Help for businesses wishing to set up in, expand in or move to areas where steel industry jobs have been lost.

Business Links; 0345 567765, for details of your local office.

Business Links is a nationwide network of 'one-stop shops', providing comprehensive, local information and advice for entrepreneurs and the self-employed.

Federation of Small Businesses Ltd, 2 Catherine Place, London SW1E 6HF; 0171-233 7900

Highlands and Islands Enterprise, Bridge House, 20 Bridge Street, Inverness IV1 1QR; 01463 234171

HM Customs and Excise, Kings Beam House, Mark Lane, London EC3R 7HE; 0171-626 1515

Industrial Common Ownership Movement, Vassalli House, 20 Central Road, Leeds LS1 6DE; 0113 246 1738

Instant Muscle, 12 Hoxton Street, London N1 6NG; 0171-613 4469.

Business advice and support for new and existing businesses. Also have a distance learning pack.

Livewire, Hawthorne House, Forth Banks, Newcastle-upon-Tyne, NE1 3SG; 0191-261 5584. A scheme sponsored by Shell UK to help young entrepreneurs make a successful start in business.

Local Enterprise Agencies. Contact your local Business Links for details. See above.

Local Enterprise Company (LEC), Scotland. For your local LEC consult the telephone directory.

Northern Ireland Innovation Programme, 22 Great Victoria Street, Belfast BT2 7BJ; 01232 241619

Office of Fair Trading, Field House, Breams Buildings, London EC4A 1PR; 0171-242 2858

Prince's Youth Business Trust, 18 Park Square East, London NW1 4LH; 0171-543 1234. Help for young entrepreneurs in the form of grants and on-going training and support.

Rural Development Commission (incorporating CoSIRA), 141 Castle Street, Salisbury, Wiltshire SP1 3TP; 01722 336255

Training and Enterprise Council (TEC), England and Wales. Contact your local Business Links for details. See above.

Welsh Development Agency, Principality House, The Friary, Cardiff CF1 4AE; 0345 775577

Further Reading from Kogan Page

Be Your Own PR Man, Michael Bland, 2nd edition
Buying a Shop, A St John Price, 4th edition
Do Your Own Bookkeeping, Max Pullen
Do Your Own Market Research, P N Hague and P Jackson, 2nd edition
The Entrepreneur's Complete Self-Assessment Guide, Douglas Gray, revised edition
Financial Management for the Small Business, Colin Barrow, 3rd edition
The First 12 Months, David H Bangs
Forming a Limited Company, Patricia Clayton, 5th edition
Getting Started, Robson Rhodes, 4th edition
Getting Started in Export, Roger Bennett
Getting Started in Importing, John Wilson
Going Freelance, Godfrey Golzen, 5th edition
How to Prepare a Business Plan, Edward Blackwell, 2nd edition
Law for the Small Business, Patricia Clayton, 8th edition
Readymade Business Opportunities, Greg Clarke
Selling by Telephone, Chris de Winter, 2nd edition
The Small Business Action Kit, J Rosthorn, A Haldane, E Blackwell and J Wholey, 4th edition
Successful Marketing for the Small Business, Dave Patten, 3rd edition
Understand Your Accounts, A St John Price, 3rd edition
Working for Yourself, Godfrey Golzen, 17th edition
Your Business Start-Up Action Kit, CD-Rom
Your Home Business Action Kit, CD-Rom